A PLACE AT THE TABLE

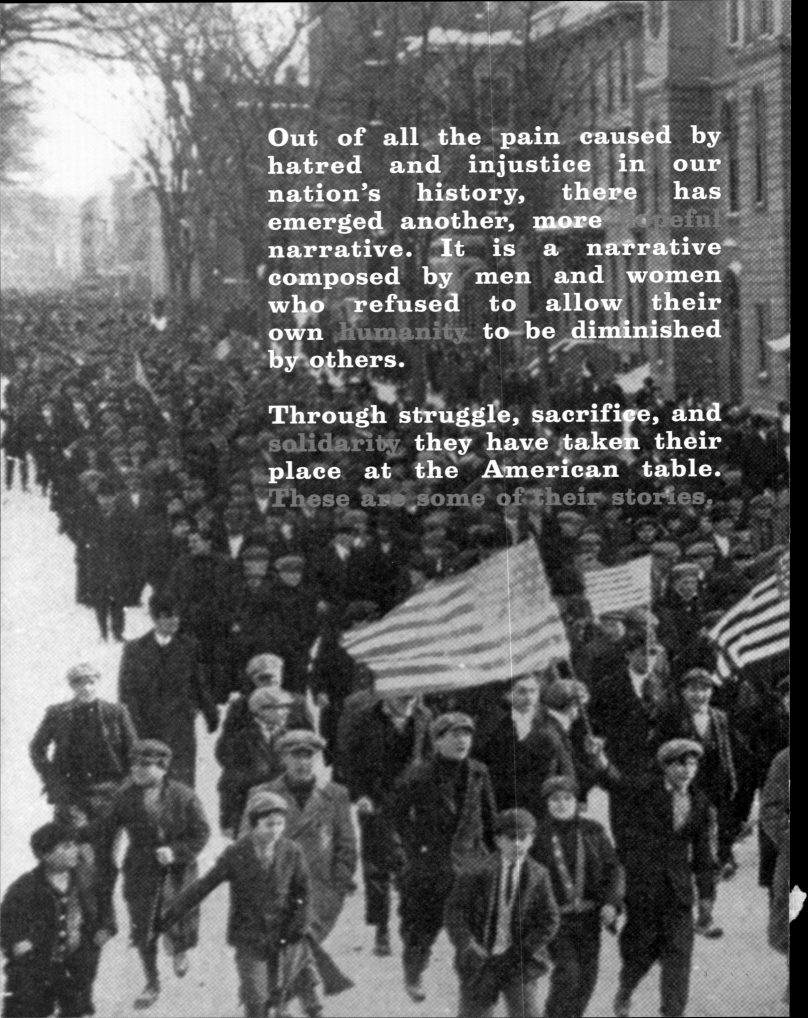

Out of all the pain caused by hatred and injustice in our nation's history, there has emerged another, more hopeful narrative. It is a narrative composed by men and women who refused to allow their own humanity to be diminished by others.

Through struggle, sacrifice, and solidarity they have taken their place at the American table. These are some of their stories.

A PLACE AT THE TABLE

Struggles for Equality in America

Edited by
MARIA FLEMING

OXFORD
UNIVERSITY PRESS

In association with the
SOUTHERN POVERTY LAW CENTER

OXFORD
UNIVERSITY PRESS

Oxford New York
Athens Auckland Bangkok Bogotá Buenos Aires Cape Town
Dar es Salaam Delhi Florence Hong Kong Istanbul Karachi
Kolkata Kuala Lumpur Madrid Melbourne Mexico City Mumbai Nairobi
Paris São Paulo Shanghai Singapore Taipei Tokyo Toronto Warsaw

and associated companies in
Berlin Ibadan

Copyright © 2001
Published by Oxford University Press
198 Madison Avenue, New York, New York 10016

Library of Congress Cataloging-in-Publication Data
A place at the table: struggles for equality in America / edited by Maria Fleming.
Includes bibliographical references and index.
Summary: Examines the efforts of many different people in American history to
secure equal treatment in such areas as religion, voting rights, education, housing,
and employment.
ISBN 0-19-515036-8
1. Civil rights--United States--History--Juvenile literature. 2. Equality--United
States--History--Juvenile literature. [1. Civil rights--History.] I. Fleming, Maria.

JC599.U5 P5 2001
323'.0973--dc21   2001036501

1 3 5 7 9 8 6 4 2
Printed in Hong Kong
on acid-free paper

CONTENTS

★ ★ ★ ★ ★ ★ ★ ★

Introduction   9

MARIA FLEMING

1 Apostles of Liberty   10

HARRIET SIGERMAN

1768: Virginia Baptists challenge the state church in the
name of religious freedom.

2 Who Claims Me?   22

GARY COLLISON

1851: Anti-slavery activists in Boston take a stand
against the Fugitive Slave Law.

3 Freedom's Main Line   34

MARIA FLEMING

1870: Black citizens of Louisville, Ky., use civil disobedience to protest segregation on public streetcars.

4 This Land Is Ours   46

BRANDON MARIE MILLER

1877: A leader of the Ponca tribe in Nebraska champions
his people's right to their ancestral home.

5 The Strike for Three Loaves   56

MARIA FLEMING

1912: Immigrant laborers in a Massachusetts mill town
join forces to demand fair pay for a day's work.

6 Road Trip for Suffrage   68

HARRIET SIGERMAN

1915: Three activists embark on a daring cross-country
journey in support of women's voting rights.

7 **The House on Lemon Street** 80

MARIA FLEMING

> 1916: A Riverside, Calif., family battles unjust laws aimed at immigrants of Japanese ancestry.

8 **A Tale of Two Schools** 90

MARIA FLEMING

> 1945: Mexican American parents in Westminster, Calif., struggle to overturn the policy of school segregation.

9 **Against the Current** 100

BETH HEGE PIATOTE

> 1974: Native Americans claim their treaty fishing rights in the Pacific Northwest.

10 **Wheels of Justice** 110

LISA BENNETT

> 1977: Disability rights activists stage a month-long sit-in at a government building in San Francisco.

11 **Going to Bat for Girls** 120

LISA BENNETT

> 1992: A Nebraska farm family questions the tradition of gender inequity in school sports.

12 **The Battle of Spanish Fork** 130

LISA BENNETT

> 1997: A gay Utah educator fights for her right to teach.

Afterword: Becoming America 142

MARIA FLEMING

Contributors 143

Further Reading 144

Index 149

A PLACE AT THE TABLE

I, Too

I, too, sing America.

I am the darker brother.
They send me to eat in the kitchen
When company comes,
But I laugh,
And eat well,
And grow strong.

Tomorrow,
I'll be at the table
When company comes.
Nobody'll dare
Say to me,
"Eat in the kitchen,"
Then.

Besides,
They'll see how beautiful I am
And be ashamed —

I, too, am America.

— *Langston Hughes*

INTRODUCTION

by MARIA FLEMING

In his poem "I, Too," Langston Hughes described how it felt to be a black man living in the United States during the first part of the 20th century. But his words speak to the experience of all groups who have been pushed to the margins of American society. They also give voice to a sustaining conviction — that true equality will come.

Out of all the pain caused by exclusion, hatred and injustice in our nation's history, there has emerged another, more hopeful narrative. This narrative has been composed by the men and women who, when told by the larger society to "stay in their place," insisted that "their place" was at the American table.

Some of these champions of justice are well known, their struggles well chronicled: Roger Williams founded the first colony based on the principle of religious freedom in the early 1600s; Susan B. Anthony and Elizabeth Cady Stanton inaugurated a half-century-long struggle for women's voting rights; Martin Luther King Jr. stirred the conscience of our country with his vision of racial justice, galvanizing the Civil Rights Movement of the 1950s and '60s; César Chávez and Dolores Huerta organized labor strikes and boycotts to advance economic justice for Mexican American farm workers, inspiring a wave of Chicano activism in the 1960s and '70s.

The lives and work of other American freedom fighters are less familiar to us, their stories overlooked or forgotten. This volume examines the courageous efforts of some of these unsung heroes who toppled barriers in education, voting, employment, housing and other areas in order to participate more fully in our democracy.

For example, in "Freedom's Main Line," you'll read about a man named Robert Fox who led a successful movement to desegregate transportation in Louisville, Kentucky, almost a century before Rosa Parks sparked the Montgomery Bus Boycott in 1955. "A Tale of Two Schools" tells the story of the Méndez family, who waged a battle against the segregated schooling of Chicano children at the same time African Americans were fighting the color line in education during the 1940s and '50s.

In addition, you'll find here the stories of women and men who crossed ethnic, racial, religious and other divides to help further the cause of justice: a Christian legislator in Maryland who risked his political career to secure equal rights for his state's Jewish population; white Americans who defended Native American land titles; gay, lesbian and black activists who lent their support to Americans with disabilities seeking access to public facilities.

As Americans, we are justly proud of the ideals of freedom, democracy and equality that are enshrined in our nation's founding documents — the Declaration of Independence, Constitution and Bill of Rights. Our challenge is to make them more than promises on paper. The stories you are about to read show how some ordinary Americans made those promises come alive, not just for themselves but for us all. ▨

1

Spotsylvania County, Virginia ❧ 1768

APOSTLES OF LIBERTY

In the United States, we often take for granted our right to worship as we please or not at all. Religious freedom is guaranteed in the First Amendment to the Constitution. But this right did not always exist. Before the American Revolution, most of the colonies had established an official Christian denomination, which all residents were required to support.

In Virginia, the Church of England (also called the Anglican Church) was the established form of Christianity, and it was supported through public taxation. But as new religious ideas and groups came to Virginia, dissenters began to question both the practices and power of the Anglican Church.

The Separate Baptists were one religious sect that challenged the authority of the established church. As a result, Separate Baptist preachers were brutally attacked throughout the colony. But from their persecution was born a remarkable contribution to the quest for religious freedom in Virginia and, ultimately, in the newly independent nation.

by **HARRIET SIGERMAN**

On June 4, 1768, John Waller, Lewis Craig and three other men stood before a magistrate in a courthouse in Spotsylvania County, Virginia. Their crime: disturbing the peace by preaching the tenets of their faith.

The men were Separate Baptists, religious dissenters who posed a threat to the colony's established church, the Church of England. The Separates were widely reviled for their religious zeal and earnest appeals to follow both the letter and spirit of the Gospel. As the attorney who prosecuted them declared, "These men . . . cannot meet a man upon the road but they must ram a text of scripture down his throat."

The jury sentenced the defendants to jail but offered to release them if they promised not to preach in the county for a year and a day. Waller, Craig and one other Separate minister refused. They were promptly led to the jailhouse in nearby

Fredericksburg. As the preachers walked through the streets, they sang a hymn:

Broad is the road that leads to death,
And thousands walk together there;
But wisdom shows a narrow path,
With here and there a traveler.

Their voices, filled with passion and conviction, aroused curiosity and sympathy among spectators. People murmured words of encouragement for the three brave men who were willing to go to prison for their right to preach and worship as they saw fit.

For 43 days, the preachers remained in the stone prison, crowded together in a tiny cell. But even imprisonment could not silence them, and the ministers continued to preach through the small grated window of their cell. Every day, people swarmed around the window to hear them. Rabble-

(Left) Large crowds would camp out all night to hear the fiery Baptist preachers. (Right) The Anglican Church governed every aspect of life in colonial Virginia.

rousers tried to drive the crowds away or sang obscene songs to drown out the preachers' words, but the faithful continued to flock to the jail-house window.

It was ironic that John Waller found himself sharing a jail cell with Lewis Craig. Just two years earlier, Craig had been the first Separate Baptist preacher arrested for "unlawful preaching" in Virginia, and Waller sat on the jury that decided his fate. At the time, Waller was a member of the Church of England. Like other Anglicans, he detested the Separate Baptists and everything they stood for.

The two religious sects could not have been more different. Transplanted by the first English settlers to Virginia and to other Southern colonies, the Anglican Church governed every aspect of colonial life. Colonists were required to attend Sunday services and to contribute corn and tobacco, as well as livestock, to support the church. Anglican services were elaborate and formal and did not encourage personal involvement.

Nor were the Anglicans known for being very devout. Many — including John Waller — enjoyed a festive social life of drinking, gambling and merrymaking. In fact, Waller so enjoyed a night of carousing that he was sometimes called the "Devil's Adjutant (assistant)" and had earned the nickname "Swearing Jack Waller."

Anglicans believed that men of wealth and power should govern, and more affluent parishioners occupied the best pews in the churches. Waller himself came from a wealthy, long-established English family and enjoyed an esteemed position within the church. Because many planters and other slaveowners were Anglican, the church did not condemn the practice of slavery.

In appearance, conduct and religious beliefs, the Separate Baptists were the antithesis of the Anglicans. Extremely pious, the Separate Baptists rejected all frivolous activity such as drinking and gambling. Furthermore, in their fellowship, every member prayed as an equal without regard to social or economic rank. This more democratic form of worship stood in stark contrast to Anglican elitism, and it greatly appealed to less educated and more humble rural colonists.

Most troubling to the Anglicans, the Separate Baptists strongly condemned slavery and invited black slaves to join their churches as equal members — a practice that stirred up planters' fears of slave revolts. Women also played prominent roles in Separate Baptist church services. The equal position of women and slaves within the Separate Baptist flock challenged the Anglican planters' social and political power over both groups.

Separate Baptist beliefs and practices were an affront to John Waller's privileged social position and to the unsavory pleasures he pursued. So when Lewis Craig was brought before the Spotsylvania County Court in 1766, it hardly seems likely that Waller could have been an impartial juror.

Perhaps fully prepared to convict Craig, Waller was instead mesmerized by the preacher's eloquent defense of himself. Craig addressed the jury: "I thank you, gentlemen of the grand jury, for the honor you have done me. While I was wicked and injurious, you took no notice of me, but since I have altered my course of life and endeavored to reform my neighbors, you concern yourselves much about me."

To Waller, Craig possessed astonishing serenity and devotion, and he wondered if he could ever achieve a similar state of grace. He began attending a Separate Baptist church and gave up drinking

A Woman Not Fit for Our Society

Puritans in colonial Massachusetts had left England to escape religious oppression, only to establish their own equally stringent theocracy in America. In the new colony, as in England, religious dissenters were jailed, beaten and sometimes even killed.

Anne Hutchinson considered herself a devout Puritan, not a dissenter. However, she interpreted the church's teachings differently than most of the Puritan ministers in Massachusetts. She began to hold informal weekly meetings where church members could discuss and debate church scripture. At first the meetings were attended only by women, who were not allowed to participate in the theological discussions that followed regular Sunday services. But soon men in the colony came to hear Hutchinson as well. Her intelligence and eloquence often attracted large crowds.

In 1637, civil and church leaders charged Hutchinson with promoting false doctrine. They also accused her of stepping beyond the church's established bounds for women, who were supposed to be seen and not heard. She was brought before Boston's General Court.

During her trial, Hutchinson insisted on her right to practice her faith according to the dictates of her conscience. The court ruled against her. Pregnant with her 16th child, she was imprisoned and later banished from Massachusetts. The following spring, she settled in the newly established colony of Rhode Island, which had been founded on the principle of religious freedom three years earlier by another religious exile from Massachusetts — Roger Williams.

Mr. Winthrop, governor: Mrs. Hutchinson, you are called here as one of those that have troubled the peace of the commonwealth and the churches here. . . . you have maintained a meeting and an assembly in your house that hath been condemned by the general assembly as a thing not tolerable nor comely in the sight of God nor fitting for your sex. . . .

Mrs. Hutchinson: What have I said or done?

Gov: Why for your doings, this you did harbour and countenance those that are parties in this faction* that you have heard of.

Mrs. H: That's [a] matter of conscience, Sir.

Gov: Your conscience you must keep or it must be kept for you. . . . Why do you keep such a meeting at your house as you do every week upon a set day?

Mrs. H: It is lawful for me so to do, as it is all your practices and can you find a warrant for yourself and condemn me for the same thing? . . .

Deputy Gov: [I]t appears by this woman's meeting that Mrs. Hutchinson hath so forestalled the minds of many . . . that now she hath a potent party in the country. Now if all these things have endangered us as from that foundation and if she in particular hath disparaged all our ministers in the land . . . we must take away the foundation and the building will fall. . . .

Mrs. H: [I]f you do condemn me for speaking what in my conscience I know to be truth I must commit myself unto the Lord. . . . You have power over my body but the Lord Jesus hath power over my body and soul, and assure yourselves thus much, you do as much as in you lies to put the Lord Jesus Christ from you, and if you go on in this course you begin you will bring a curse upon you and your posterity, and the mouth of the Lord hath spoken it. . . . [N]ow having seen him which is invisible I fear not what man can do unto me. . . .

Gov: The court hath already declared themselves satisfied concerning things you hear, and concerning the troublesomeness of her spirit and the danger of her course amongst us, which is not to be suffered. . . . Mrs. Hutchinson, the sentence of the court you hear is that you are banished from out of our jurisdiction as being a woman not fit for our society, and are to be imprisoned till the court shall send you away.

* *Hutchinson was accused of associating with the much-despised antinomians, who believed that Christians were not bound by church law.*

Itinerant preachers often baptized dozens of people at each stop on their journey.

and gambling, but he despaired of ever achieving religious salvation. One day, after witnessing another person's conversion, he fled into some nearby woods and dropped to his knees, pleading for a sign of divine mercy. Finally it came. "In an instant I felt my heart melt," he later reported, "and a sweet application of the Redeemer's love to my poor soul. The calm was great but short."

In 1767, Waller was baptized and became a Separate Baptist preacher — a religious leader of a group he once despised. It was a choice that would bring him spiritual fulfillment, but at a cost, for in colonial Virginia, Waller's new vocation was a dangerous profession.

Still, Waller's arrest in 1768 did not dampen his eagerness to spread the gospel. After his release from prison, Waller redoubled his efforts to preach and convert others. The Separate Baptist movement was a traveling ministry, and Waller and his fellow preachers held meetings almost every day in Spotsylvania and neighboring counties. The preachers logged hundreds of miles, often on foot, to seek out new members. Despite the scorn of the established church, the Separates' message quickly took root in many parts of Virginia. Hundreds of people would camp out all night to hear Waller and other ministers preach the following day. In sparsely settled regions, people eagerly traveled 100 miles or more to attend their meetings.

Unlike the Anglicans, the Separate Baptists did not baptize children. Instead they believed that baptism should be a voluntary conversion experience reserved for those who were spiritually prepared. The itinerant preachers sometimes baptized as many

> The equal position of women and slaves within the Separate Baptist flock challenged the Anglican planters' social and political power over both groups.

A Question of Faith

When the U.S. Constitution was adopted in 1788, guaranteeing Americans religious freedom, many states were imposing "religious tests" for those who wanted to hold public office or practice law. These tests required individuals to profess a belief in Jesus Christ. Although the Constitution forbade such tests for federal office, states still could require them for their political leaders. Gradually, however, states abandoned these religious constraints in keeping with the democratic spirit of the times.

Maryland was the last state to waive its religious test. For 30 years, the state's small Jewish population petitioned against the discriminatory law without success. But in 1817, Jews found an ally in a Christian state legislator named Thomas Kennedy who was willing to risk his political career to champion the cause of religious liberty.

The fact that he was not acquainted with any of Maryland's Jews did not deter Kennedy from fighting for their rights. Although there were only about 150 Jews in Maryland at the time, Kennedy believed,

Thomas Kennedy

> [I]f there was only one — to that one, we ought to do justice. . . . Numbers cannot make a difference as to the principle, for if a single member of the body or the body politic suffer, the whole body suffers also. If one citizen is denied the enjoyment of his rights today, numbers may be tomorrow, until at last the whole community may be reduced to a state of abject slavery.

It became Kennedy's obsession, a very peculiar one in the eyes of many, to eliminate the legally enforced prejudice against this almost invisible group of Marylanders.

He became the subject of jest among his fellow legislators, the butt of jokes.

But Kennedy would not be quieted. He kept pressing to have passed what he titled "An Act to extend to the sect of people professing the Jewish religion the same rights and privileges that are enjoyed by Christians." At one House of Delegates session after another, the measure was voted down.

Undeterred, Kennedy continued to deliver impassioned speeches to the state Assembly promoting the bill. In one address, he spoke movingly of the sad legacy of prejudice, which must be acknowledged and then abandoned:

> There is only one opponent that I fear at this time, and that is PREJUDICE — our prejudices . . . are dear to us, we all know and feel the force of our political prejudices, but our religious prejudices are still more strong, still more dear; they cling to us through life, and scarcely leave us on the bed of death, and it is not the prejudice of a generation, of an age or of a century, that we have now to encounter. No, it is the prejudice which has passed from father to son, for almost eighteen hundred years. . . .
>
> Perhaps I have . . . seen and felt more of the effects of religious prejudice [in my native Scotland] than most of the members of this house. I once had a father who was a strict and undeviating Christian in his walk and conversation, and who would not have injured his neighbor for the wealth of the world; yet that father with all his piety, was so wedded to his Presbyterian opinions that he would rather have followed his twelve

children to the grave, than seen one of them turn Roman Catholic; a hereditary hatred had subsisted for ages between those sects. . . .

I never expect to be so good a man as my father, but having seen so many more Catholics than he, and having been intimate with many of them, and having found them as amiable in all respects as the professors of other doctrines — my prejudice against them, if ever I had any, is forever at an end.

His opponents in the Assembly denounced Kennedy as an "enemy of Christianity," a "Judas," mounting "a shameful attack upon the Christian religion"; he was voted out of office. But that didn't end his crusade. "Although exiled at home, I shall continue to battle for the measure, aye, until my last drop of blood," Kennedy vowed.

And continue to fight he did. As time passed, others gradually joined Kennedy in promoting the cause of religious freedom, some of them prominent Maryland citizens. In 1825, Kennedy was returned to office and reintroduced his bill. Finally, the measure passed — nearly a decade after Kennedy had first introduced it. The victory was, a jubilant Kennedy wrote to a friend, the realization of his dearest wish.

Eight years after the bill became law, Kennedy died in a cholera epidemic at the age of 55, and his crusade for justice gradually faded from memory. But in 1918, a hundred years after Kennedy introduced the bill, a retired state representative named E. Milton Altfeld heard about his battle for religious liberty. Altfeld, himself a Jew, was fascinated and moved by the story of a Christian man who devoted much of his political life to defending the rights of people who practiced a religion different from his own. The former legislator led a fundraising campaign among Maryland's Jewish community to build a monument to Kennedy. Today it stands over the spot where Kennedy lies buried. On the tall column is written:

❧ TO ONE WHO LOVED HIS FELLOW MAN ❧

as 200 during each journey they made. Waller himself would baptize more than 2,000 people into the faith during his career as a minister.

To their critics, the Separate Baptists were a dour, humorless lot who solemnly addressed each other as "Brother" and "Sister." Yet in their church services, the Separate Baptists were anything but melancholy. Unlike the more subdued Anglicans, the Separates expressed their religious devotion with astonishing emotional outbursts. Members cried out, fell to the ground or leapt into the air in a religious frenzy. Some bawled while others barked like dogs, and still others became temporarily paralyzed, so intense was the power of their religious devotion.

To outsiders, they presented an alarming sight in the zeal and fervor of their worshiping. Some observers scoffed that they were merely pretending, but others feared that demons had possessed the Separates. They were, according to a woman who lived near one congregation, an "outlandish set of people."

But it was neither the Separate Baptists' impassioned form of worship nor their earnest, dour manner that alarmed defenders of the traditional order. Instead, it was the Separates' rejection of the hierarchical standards of society, especially their opposition to slavery and their refusal to abide by the law.

Other Baptist sects and dissenters from the Anglican Church complied with the Act of Toleration of 1689. This act granted dissenters the right to preach if they obtained special licenses from colonial authorities. The Separate Baptists, however, refused to follow this law, firmly believing in their divinely ordained right to preach whenever and wherever they wanted — including the town square.

The courageous resolve of Waller and other preachers brought fierce harassment and persecution. At first, other colonists, rather than government officials, tried to silence these blasphemers of the official church.

As soon as Separate Baptist preachers began to speak, mobs of angry colonists — mostly men — attacked them with clubs or kicked and cuffed them. To disrupt meetings, people threw live snakes and hornets' nests into crowds of listeners gathered around preachers or jeered and shouted at the top of their lungs to drown out the preachers' words. When preachers conducted baptisms by immersing converts in a lake or pond, men on horseback often rode right into the middle of the baptisms to stop them. Some men dragged the ministers into the water while they were preaching and even tried to drown them.

James Reed, an early Separate Baptist preacher, was once pulled off a stage while preaching and was kicked and beaten by ruffians. Another, Richard Major, was nearly pummeled by a mob until a pair of brothers, who had earlier heard him preach, rescued him. Less fortunate another time, Major was brutally attacked by a man with a club. But he reportedly fended off his assailant with these words: "Satan, I command thee to come out of the man." And the attacker stopped.

As the Separate Baptists gained more adherents, assaults against them turned into government-sponsored persecution. Colonial authorities threatened them with arrest as "disturbers of the peace"

and ordered them to stop preaching or face imprisonment. The Separates stubbornly refused and went to jail. John Waller was arrested repeatedly and spent more than 100 days in jail for preaching his beliefs.

When the threat of imprisonment failed to deter Separate preachers, Anglican leaders and government officials also turned to violence. In the spring of 1771, as John Waller stood on a stage reciting a psalm in a village in Caroline County, Virginia, the Anglican minister of the parish, his clerk and the sheriff barged in. With his riding crop, the minister tried to knock Waller's Bible out of his hands, but Waller held on tightly and managed to finish the psalm.

Then, as he began to pray, the minister rammed the butt of his crop into Waller's mouth to silence him. His clerk grabbed Waller and dragged him over to the sheriff. While the clerk held Waller

That the Oppressed May Go Free

Virginia's Baptists flooded the state assembly with petitions entreating lawmakers to guarantee religious equality. In 1776, they submitted their largest petition, which was signed by 10,000 Baptists, Presbyterians, Quakers, Mennonites and other religious dissenters in the state, pressing for disestablishment of the tax-supported Church of England and asking that all religious denominations enjoy the same freedoms and privileges.

To the Honourable the President and House of Delegates

The Petition of the Dissenters from the Ecclesiastical establishment in the Commonwealth of Virginia

Humbly sheweth
That your Petitioners being in common with the other Inhabitants of this Commonwealth delivered from British Oppression rejoice in the Prospect of having their Freedom

secured and maintained to them and their posterity inviolate. The hopes of your petitioners have been raised and confirmed by the Declaration of your Honourable House with regard to equal Liberty. Equal Liberty! that invaluable blessing: which though it be the birth right of every good Member of the State has been what your Petitioners have been Deprived of, in that, by Taxation their property hath been wrested from them and given to those from whom they have received no equivalent.

Your Petitioners therefore having long groaned under the Burden of an Ecclesiastical Establishment beg leave to move your Honourable House that this as well as every other Yoke may be broken and that the Oppressed may go free: that so every religious Denomination being on a Level, Animosities may cease, and that Christian Forbearance, Love and Charity, may be practised towards each other, while the Legislature interferes only to support them in their just Rights and equal privileges.

down, the sheriff took a whip and proceeded to give Waller 20 lashes, although he lacked any warrant for his arrest or other authorization to punish him. Bloody and lacerated but undefeated, Waller limped back to his audience and courageously preached a sermon.

All told, some 50 preachers were jailed or attacked during this period of religious turmoil in Virginia. But the Separates could not be beaten into silence. Such persecution only increased their yearnings for religious freedom.

Their belief in religious freedom made the Separate Baptists ardent supporters of the American Revolution. Starting in 1775, while their fellow colonists timidly debated the merits of war, Separate Baptist ministers clamored for independence from Great Britain. They envisioned a new nation in which religious freedom was the law of the land and citizens were no longer compelled to support an established church through taxes.

In fact, the Revolution itself — with its central ideals of liberty and autonomy — created a climate that favored religious freedom. As Virginia moved from colony to state in the newly independent nation, its ties with the "Mother Country," including the Church of England, began to weaken. And the Separate Baptists' long-held hope of religious liberty was finally gaining widespread support.

> **The Separates could not be beaten into silence.**

Now, the Separates had some important allies in their cause. Among them was the influential Virginia leader and future U.S. president James Madison. Like the Separates, Madison believed that people should be free to worship according to the dictates of their conscience.

As a young man, Madison had visited a group of Baptist ministers imprisoned in Culpeper County, Virginia, for preaching. Shocked by the crude, crowded jail conditions and by such blatant attempts to muffle them, he reportedly promised the preachers, "I shall not be silenced." Still haunted by his visit to the jailhouse, Madison later wrote a friend, "It's a good thing that the Church of England was not established throughout the colonies. That diabolical, hell-conceived

The emotional fervor of Baptist worship services presented an alarming sight to outsiders.

principle of persecution rages.... Pray for liberty of conscience."

But Madison did more than pray. Along with Thomas Jefferson, the author of the Declaration of Independence and another strong proponent of religious liberty, he pushed for legislation to guarantee that freedom. Meanwhile, the Separate Baptists and other religious dissenters circulated petitions throughout the state urging that "the church establishment should be abolished, and religion left to stand upon its own merits, and [that] all religious societies should be protected in the peaceable enjoyment of their own religious principles and modes of worship." This was a clarion call for religious freedom and for the separation of church and state.

It would take another decade of lobbying by Madison and continued pressure from the Baptists and other dissenters, but on January 16, 1786, the Virginia Statute for Religious Freedom — drafted by Jefferson eight years earlier and submitted by Madison to the General Assembly — became law. The freedom to worship without fear of imprisonment or other legal penalties was now guaranteed to all of Virginia's citizens.

Four years later, Virginia's religious freedom clause would be encoded in the First Amendment to the United States Constitution. And the Separate Baptists' long, arduous struggle for religious freedom — a struggle that resulted in the complete separation of church and state — finally bore fruit in that shining beacon of American liberty, the Bill of Rights. ☒

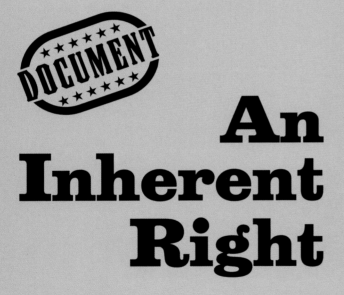

DOCUMENT

An Inherent Right

While the Constitution guaranteed most Americans the freedom to worship as they pleased when it was ratified in 1788, Native Americans had to wait nearly 200 more years before the U.S. government acknowledged their right to religious freedom. Before that, Indians were frequently denied access to sacred sites, including ancient burial grounds. The use of certain sacred objects was prohibited and some sacred ceremonies were banned. In 1978, Congress passed the Indian Religious Freedom Act with the intention of ending a history of intolerance toward Native religions.

Whereas the freedom of religion for all people is an inherent right, fundamental to the democratic structure of the United States and is guaranteed by the First Amendment of the United States Constitution;

Whereas the United States has traditionally rejected the concept of a government denying individuals the right to practice their religion and, as a result, has benefited from a rich variety of religious heritages in this country;

Whereas the religious practices of the American Indian (as well as Native Alaskan and Hawaiian) are an integral part of their culture, tradition and heritage, such practices forming the basis of Indian identity and value systems; . . .

Whereas the lack of a clear, comprehensive, and consistent Federal policy has often resulted in the abridgment of religious freedom for traditional American Indians;

Whereas such religious infringements result from the lack of knowledge or the insensitive and inflexible enforcement of Federal policies and regulations premised on a variety of laws;

. . . Now, therefore, be it

Resolved by the Senate and House of Representatives of the United States of America in Congress assembled, That henceforth it shall be the policy of the United States to protect and preserve for American Indians their inherent right of freedom to believe, express, and exercise the traditional religions of the American Indian, Eskimo, Aleut, and Native Hawaiians, including but not limited to access to sites, use and possession of sacred objects, and the freedom to worship through ceremonials and traditional rites.

Breaking New Ground

The first Muslim families in Quincy, Massachusetts, settled there in the 1930s. The local congregation established a mosque in the early 1960s and grew over the next 30 years to include more than 500 members. The joyous process of planning a new, larger worship center in Milton, Massachusetts, took a somber turn in 1991 when local residents altered zoning provisions and parking restrictions and used other legal maneuvers to block purchase of the building site.

After filing a civil rights lawsuit, the Muslim community decided to change its strategy and focus on the future. Almost immediately, a couple from Sharon, a predominantly Jewish town nearby, extended an offer to sell the group their farm. The Sharon clergy association soon added its voice to the welcome. What had become an experience of discouragement and discrimination was transformed once again — into an affirmation of religious diversity. The following article covering the groundbreaking ceremony for the new mosque appeared in The Boston Globe *on April 3, 1993.*

Dr. Mian Ashraf, president of the Islamic Center of New England, scanned the makeshift tent protecting the crowd from a frigid, steady drizzle.

He saw a Greek Orthodox bishop and a Catholic bishop, Jesuit priests and Protestant ministers. He saw enough rabbis to field a basketball team. He saw Talal Eid, imam of his congregation, and a host of other Muslim ministers. And he had to smile.

"I thought all these religious leaders might be able to arrange some better weather than this," said Ashraf, beaming like a proud father.

Pillars of the Muslim, Christian and Jewish communities came together for yesterday's groundbreaking of the Islamic Center's new Sharon headquarters.

The buzzwords of the day were harmony, unity, peace, strength, mutual respect, common ground. And the mood was positively giddy.

"Welcome to Sharon: the New Jerusalem," Eid crowed.

For Ashraf, Eid and the rest of their 500-member congregation, the ceremony marked a triumphant milestone in a long search for a new home. The congregation has outgrown its Quincy Point headquarters and now intends to build a new school for religious instruction, a social hall and eventually a mosque on its 55-acre Sharon property, a former horse farm off Chase Drive. But there were times not long ago when center officials wondered if this day would ever come.

Last year, they thought they had reached a deal with the Assumptionist Fathers, a Roman Catholic order, to buy a 7 1/2-acre property on Adams Street in Milton. The deal fell through at the last minute when five local opponents of the center bought the property themselves, leading the center to file a discrimination suit.

But congregation leaders dropped the suit, preferring to continue their search for a community where they were welcome. They found that welcome in Sharon, a quiet suburb with a sizeable Christian community and an even larger Jewish population.

"We've had a wonderful reception in Sharon," Ashraf said. "Our new neighbors have welcomed us with open arms. That doesn't happen very often."

Yesterday afternoon, speaker after speaker stood upon a wobbly chair to salute Ashraf and praise his vision of interfaith harmony. Holy men, politicians, diplomats, youth workers, professors — even the center's cook said a few words. They quoted the Koran, the Torah and the New Testament. The metaphors varied, but the message stayed the same.

"We are truly breaking ground today," said Rabbi Barry Starr of Sharon. "We're breaking new ground for a new community."

— Excerpted with permission of The Boston Globe

2

From the beginning of the slave trade in the colonies, black women and men rebelled against the brutal institution. In the fields, slaves engaged in passive resistance by refusing to work. Some organized armed uprisings. Many followed the abolitionist advice to "vote for freedom with their feet" by fleeing their masters.

By the mid-19th century, thousands of slaves were escaping each year on the legendary Underground Railroad. To appease Southern slaveholders, Congress passed a harsh new Fugitive Slave Law in 1850. The measure obligated all citizens to aid federal agents in recapturing runaways and imposed severe penalties on anyone assisting escaped slaves. Black abolitionists — many of whom were former slaves themselves — joined with their white allies to vehemently denounce the measure.

In Boston, widely regarded as the center of the abolition movement, black leaders called on citizens "to trample this law underfoot" and "to make Massachusetts a battlefield in defense of liberty." It wouldn't take long before they had a chance to act on their pledge of resistance.

by **GARY COLLISON**

WHO CLAIMS ME?

In Boston, the 15th of February, 1851, was a dreary, rain-drenched day in the middle of a winter thaw. At the Cornhill Coffee House in the heart of downtown, young Shadrach Minkins bent over his early morning customers as they sipped their coffee. A fugitive slave from Norfolk, Virginia, Minkins had escaped to Boston only nine months before. He had been lucky to find this job as a waiter at one of the city's most popular restaurants soon after arriving.

Almost unnoticed, a group of men slipped into the room. As they strode straight toward him, Minkins had an uneasy feeling. Suddenly, their hands reached out, encircling his arms and wrists, pinning them at his sides. Minkins struggled, but he was alone and they were many. They dragged him to the doorway, then out into the muddy street, walking rapidly with him in their midst.

This was the nightmare moment that every fugitive slave feared, the moment when the world came crashing down, when the trap closed, and terror and confusion reigned.

For Shadrach Minkins and Boston's other estimated 400 to 600 fugitive slaves, a dire moment such as this had been looming over them ever since the enactment of the Fugitive Slave Law the previous September. Before the new law, no Northern city had seemed safer than Boston, which was known since the days of the American Revolution for its commitment to human liberty.

It is true that the system of slavery had so poisoned race relations, both North and South, that many white Bostonians refused to accept African Americans as equals — or even to accommodate them at all — in restaurants, theaters and even, in a few notorious instances, in churches. Some white Bostonians thought that fugitive slaves had no right to live in their city and should be sent back to the South.

Still, many white Bostonians sympathized with the plight of fugitive slaves. The last fugitive slave arrested in Boston had been George Latimer in 1843, and he had been released after antislavery activists forced the man who claimed him as his property to accept a purchase price well below market value. Since then, Boston's fugitive slaves had been sleeping pretty soundly at night.

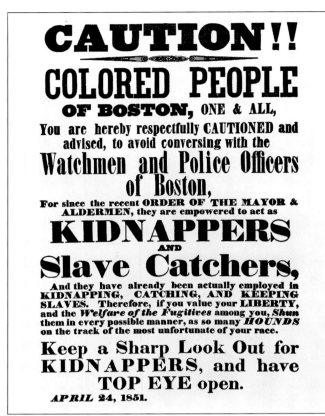

CAUTION!!

COLORED PEOPLE OF BOSTON, ONE & ALL,

You are hereby respectfully CAUTIONED and advised, to avoid conversing with the

Watchmen and Police Officers of Boston,

For since the recent ORDER OF THE MAYOR & ALDERMEN, they are empowered to act as

KIDNAPPERS

AND

Slave Catchers,

And they have already been actually employed in KIDNAPPING, CATCHING, AND KEEPING SLAVES. Therefore, if you value your LIBERTY, and the *Welfare of the Fugitives* among you, *Shun* them in every possible manner, as so many *HOUNDS* on the track of the most unfortunate of your race.

Keep a Sharp Look Out for KIDNAPPERS, and have TOP EYE open.

APRIL 24, 1851.

But the new law had changed everything. It was part of the package of legislation known as the Compromise of 1850, designed to heal the growing rift between the North and the South. The South agreed to allow Western territories to come into the Union as free states if the citizens of those states chose to do so. In exchange, the South got a Fugitive Slave Law that had real teeth in it.

The law created special commissioners to hear fugitive slave cases and authorized the U.S. marshal to employ an army of deputies to aid in the slave's return. Anyone caught helping a fugitive slave to escape faced thousands of dollars in fines and as many as six months in jail.

In effect, the U.S. Congress had traded away the hard-won freedom of fugitive slaves for peace between the North and the South. The law posed

> This was the nightmare moment that every fugitive slave feared.

(*Above left*) Around Boston, abolitionists posted notices warning blacks to beware of slave catchers. (*Above*) Boston authorities broke up this abolitionist meeting on December 3, 1860.

a threat to free blacks as well as fugitives, since anyone could claim that a man or woman was a runaway. Blacks taken into custody could not testify on their own behalf in court and were denied a trial by jury.

The law left blacks in Boston — and around the nation — exceedingly vulnerable. Would the next knock on the door be the U.S. marshal bearing a warrant for their arrest? Would they soon find themselves in Richmond, Charleston or Savannah being sold to the highest bidder on an auction block or bound to a whipping post? It was a terrifying prospect.

African Americans loudly condemned the measure. "I received my freedom from Heaven, and with it came the command to defend my title to it," declared Jermain W. Loguen, a black abolitionist minister in Syracuse, N.Y., who had fled his master in Tennessee several years earlier. "I don't respect this law — I don't fear it — I won't obey it! It outlaws me, and I outlaw it."

In the first month under the new law, newspapers carried reports of a great exodus of fugitives fleeing to Canada from Pittsburgh, Philadelphia, Cincinnati and elsewhere. In late September, the capture and re-enslavement of James Hamlet in New York City, another antislavery center, gave Boston's fugitive slaves even more reason to be frightened. Some packed a few belongings, made hasty farewells to friends and family, and disappeared into the night. Hundreds teetered on the verge of flight.

The alarm had been sounded. Meanwhile, Boston's black leaders strategized about how best to protect runaways and attack the new law.

No one knew better than Lewis Hayden, an antislavery leader and fugitive slave himself, what this time of crisis required. Six years before, hidden in a carriage driven by two abolitionist friends, Hayden had escaped from Kentucky with his wife and son. They made it safely to Canada, but Hayden felt too isolated from the struggles of his fellow fugitive slaves, and the family soon moved back to the United States. In 1848, they settled in Boston with the aim of helping the city's fugitives and the abolitionist cause.

(Left) Under the Fugitive Slave Law, anyone caught helping a fugitive slave faced severe penalties. (Above) These residents of Oberlin, Ohio, were punished for helping fugitive slaves in 1859.

RAN AWAY!

FROM THE SUBSCRIBER. My Mulatto Boy, GEORGE. Said George is 5 feet 8 inches in height, brown curly Hair, dark coat. I will give $400 for him alive, and the same sum for satisfactory proof that he has been killed.

Vide ANTHONY & ELLIS' MAMMOTH "UNCLE TOM'S CABIN." WM. HARRIS.

Hayden set up shop as a clothing dealer and took up residence in the largely black West End neighborhood on Beacon Hill. The Hayden house quickly became a refuge for many a newly arrived fugitive slave and a headquarters for Boston's black activists and their allies. Harriet Beecher Stowe, author of the famous *Uncle Tom's Cabin* (1852), once found 13 fugitive slaves living under the Hayden family's roof.

Hayden remembered well the horrors of slavery. As a youth, he had witnessed the auctioning off of his brothers and sisters. He himself had been traded from one master to another for a pair of carriage horses. Twice his mother had tried to kill herself to escape the barbaric institution. No fugitive was going to be returned to slavery if Lewis Hayden could possibly help it.

Presiding at a preliminary meeting of the black community, Hayden called for "an united and persevering resistance." At a second, even larger assembly, the group adopted bold resolutions promising to defend the freedom of every fugitive slave among them, to the death if necessary. "They who would be free, themselves must strike the blow," one resolution stated. Another authorized a "League of Freedom" composed of men who, in the words of one speaker, "could do the heavy work in the hour of difficulty." Their defiant words echoed those being pronounced at similar meetings around the nation.

Other resolutions passed by Boston's black citizens warned fugitives to be cautious and to initiate no violence but, if attacked, to fight for their freedom with all their strength, with any weapon at hand. Still another resolution appealed to their many white allies in the city to rally around them in resistance to the obnoxious law.

The call for help was soon answered. On October 14, friends of Boston's fugitive slaves gathered for a meeting at Faneuil Hall, known as the "Cradle of Liberty" for all the patriot meetings held there during the Revolution. Famed abolitionist Frederick Douglass came down from Rochester, New York, to encourage the gathering with fiery words.

"We must be prepared should this law be put into operation to see the streets of Boston running with blood," Douglass warned. The meeting resulted in the formation of a new biracial organization, the Boston Vigilance Committee, to protect fugitive slaves and provide relief to destitute fugitives. As a member of the

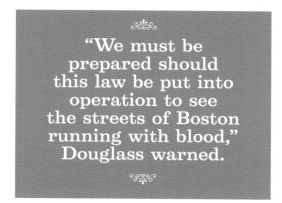

"We must be prepared should this law be put into operation to see the streets of Boston running with blood," Douglass warned.

executive committee, Lewis Hayden was to play a key role in these efforts.

Their preparations hadn't been made any too soon. At the end of October, two "man-stealing" agents for a Macon, Georgia, slaveholder arrived in Boston. They immediately set about obtaining warrants for the arrest of a fugitive slave couple, William and Ellen Craft, who lodged at Hayden's West End home.

Fortunately, federal officials were slow to act. By the time they got around to issuing warrants for the Crafts, the entire African-American 6th Ward neighborhood was armed and ready. Reports said Hayden's house had been turned into a fortress with powder kegs

DOCUMENT By Any Means Necessary

No anti-slavery publication inspired more fear in Southern slaveholders than a 76-page pamphlet known as "Walker's Appeal." Penned by black abolitionist David Walker in 1829, the powerful treatise called for the violent overthrow of slavery.

Walker, a used clothing merchant in Boston, found ways to circulate his pamphlet secretly among slaves. Southern leaders responded by passing stricter laws against teaching slaves to read. It also became a crime, punishable by death, to distribute the pamphlet in some states. The governor of Georgia offered a reward to anyone who could deliver Walker to him — dead or alive.

In his "Appeal," Walker condemned blacks for their passivity in submitting to the yoke of slavery and whites for their hypocrisy in proclaiming their love of liberty while enslaving millions of men, women and children of African descent.

Just nine months after "Walker's Appeal" was published, its author was found dead in the doorway of his clothing shop. The cause of David Walker's death was never determined, but some suspected he was poisoned.

Are we MEN!! — I ask you, O my brethren! are we *MEN?* Did our Creator make us to be slaves to dust and ashes like ourselves? Are they not dying worms as well as we? . . . How we could be so *submissive* to a gang of men, whom we cannot tell whether they are *as good* as ourselves or not, I never could conceive. . . .

Remember Americans, that we must and shall be free and enlightened as you are, will you wait until we shall, under God, obtain our liberty by the crushing arm of power? Will it not be dreadful for you? I speak Americans for your good. . . . You may do your best to keep us in wretchedness and misery, to enrich you and your children, but God will deliver us from under you. And wo, wo, will be to you if we have to obtain our freedom by fighting. Throw away your fears and prejudices then, and enlighten us and treat us like men, and we will like you more than we do now hate you. . . . America is as much our country, as it is yours.

Treat us like men, and there is no danger but we will all live in peace and happiness together. . . . But Americans, I declare to you, while you keep us and our children in bondage, and treat us like brutes, to make us support you and your families, we cannot be your friends. . . . Treat us then like men . . . [a]nd there is not a doubt in my mind, but that the whole of the past will be sunk into oblivion, and we yet, under God, will become a united and happy people.

rigged up in the basement to explode should the U.S. marshal's men break in. Unwilling to risk the lives of his officers, the marshal wisely decided to ponder his options before taking any action.

Meanwhile, the Boston Vigilance Committee harassed the slave catchers while they remained in the city. They filed lawsuits against them for petty infractions such as smoking in the street. Committee members dogged their every footstep, calling out, "Slave catchers! Slave catchers! There go the slave catchers!" Finally, after enduring a week of legal delays and relentless torment, the Georgians left town in disgust, convinced that Boston was no place for recovering runaway slaves.

Boston's black and white abolitionists were jubilant. Lewis Hayden, however, knew that their victory would not be without consequences. No longer safe in Boston, the Crafts had to be sent to England for protection. Their escape enraged Southerners and their Northern friends, including Boston businessmen who traded with the South, making other attempts on fugitives virtually inevitable. Widely denounced for incompetence, Boston's U.S. marshal and federal officials would not take such a cautious,

Revolution Within a Revolution

In 1776, while white colonists sought "a new birth of freedom" through war with Britain, they held thousands of African Americans in bondage. This cruel contradiction was not lost on black men and women, who used the principles at the heart of the American Revolution to challenge the institution of slavery.

Black activism during the Revolutionary War was particularly strong in New England, where the Patriot ideals of liberty and independence were shouted on every street corner. Seizing on this revolutionary rhetoric, African Americans presented petition after petition to state legislatures requesting emancipation.

Some African Americans during this era took their demand for liberty to the courts. A slave known as Mumbet was among a handful of blacks filing such "freedom suits" in Massachusetts.

Born around 1742 in Clavereck, New York, Mumbet came to the Bay Colony of Massachusetts as a piece of inherited property, along with her sister Lizzie. Although a much smaller percentage of the population in the North were slaves than in the South, slavery was still an established and accepted institution.

Mumbet worked as a house slave for Col. John and Hannah Ashley in Sheffield, Massachusetts. Col. Ashley was a wealthy merchant, a member of the colonial legislature and a judge. Guests to the Ashley home were equally prominent, and Mumbet often overhead the men debating political and philosophical subjects — including the war with Britain and the natural rights of man — as she served them late-night suppers.

During the winter of 1773, the men encoded their thoughts in a political statement called the Sheffield Declaration. One resolution of the declaration read: "Resolved that Mankind in a state of Nature are equal, free, and independent of each other, and have a right to the undisturbed Enjoyment of their lives, their Liberty and Property." So important was this resolution that part of it would be added to the Massachusetts state constitution a few years later.

Mumbet pondered the meaning of the ringing phrases. The words took root in her mind and, in time, would bear sweet fruit.

unhurried approach the next time a slaveholder tried to recover his property.

The "next time" came all too soon, at Boston's Cornhill Coffee House. Now it was Shadrach Minkins who found his world suddenly shattered, his freedom wrenched away in an instant. With Minkins firmly in their grasp, the federal officials rapidly reached the Boston Court House and climbed the stairs to the second floor. Minkins, still wearing his waiter's apron, struggled to understand what was happening.

"Who claims me?" he demanded, as the marshals rushed him into the U.S. courtroom where his fate would be decided.

Although the officers had made the arrest quietly, the news passed rapidly along the city's network of white and black abolitionists. Within a short time, lawyers from the Boston Vigilance Committee began arriving to take up Minkins' defense. Robert Morris, Boston's only black lawyer, soon joined the group.

It was late morning before the legal proceedings finally began. The lawyer for the Norfolk slaveholder presented a stack of legal documents proving that

One day, several years later, Mumbet's sister Lizzie baked a small bread for herself from the scrapings of the bowl used for the Ashley family's wheat cake. When Hannah Ashley smelled the bread, she became enraged at this act of "thievery." She grabbed a heated shovel from the kitchen hearth and swung it at Lizzie. Mumbet jumped between Hannah and Lizzie to defend her sister, and took a blow that burned her arm.

As soon as her injury healed, Mumbet walked out of the Ashley home and "refused the insult and outrage of slavery." She remembered the words of the Sheffield Declaration and decided that "not being a dumb beast, I had the right to be free and equal." In her years working in the home of a judge, Mumbet had learned a good deal about the Massachusetts legal system, and she decided to use the courts to "try whether I did not come among them who were free."

Mumbet and another of the colonel's slaves, a man named Brom, sought legal help in Stockbridge, Massachusetts, from a young lawyer who had been a frequent guest in the Ashley home, Theodore Sedgwick. One of the authors of the Sheffield Declaration, Sedgwick agreed to defend Elizabeth in *Brom and Bett* v. *J. Ashley, Esq.,* filed in 1781.

Col. Ashley asked the court to return his "property," claiming that he had clear legal title to them as "servants for life." In opposition to the colonel's claim, Sedgwick

Elizabeth Freeman

argued that it was Mumbet and Brom who had been deprived of property — their own persons. The judge decided in favor of the plaintiffs, and Mumbet walked out of the courtroom a free woman.

Along with other successful freedom suits, Mumbet's legal victory tolled the bells for slavery in Massachusetts. Around the same time, other Northern states were enacting laws that called for the gradual emancipation of slaves. By the 1830s, slavery was a Southern institution.

As for Mumbet, following the lawsuit she took "Elizabeth Freeman" for her name. She refused Col. Ashley's invitation to return to his home to work as a paid servant. Instead she worked for lawyer Theodore Sedgwick, nursing his sick wife and helping to raise his children.

The Sedgwick children regarded Freeman with great respect and love. Catherine Sedgwick, who became a novelist, wrote Elizabeth Freeman's biography after Freeman died around the age of 85. In that text, Sedgwick recalls the deep yearnings for liberty that had prompted her beloved friend to become a freedom fighter in America's other revolution.

Sedgwick remembers Freeman once telling her, "Anytime, anytime while I was a slave, if one minute's freedom had been offered to me, and I had been told I must die at the end of that minute, I would have taken it — just to stand one minute . . . on God's earth a free woman."

At Fortress Monroe, Va., runaway slaves appealed to federal guards for freedom and protection.

he had purchased Minkins sometime in 1849. After these documents were read, the hearing adjourned. Minkins was allowed to remain in the courtroom to consult with his lawyers.

The Rev. Leonard Grimes, the black minister of Boston's 12th Baptist Church, sometimes called "The Church of the Fugitive Slaves," came and sat beside Minkins to advise him. Grimes remembered later that the runaway's hand was shaking badly from all the excitement. The minister had to help him make his 'X' on the legal papers his lawyers placed before him.

Meanwhile, a great crowd composed mostly of African Americans had gathered in the hallway and outside in Court Square. Increasingly restless, the crowd peppered anyone who emerged from the courtroom with urgent questions. Rumors flew. According to one, Minkins was to be taken to the Federal Naval Yard. Another claimed that the U.S. Army

had been summoned, still another that Minkins was to be put aboard a ship bound for the South. If ever there was a time for Lewis Hayden and the "League of Freedom" to act, that time was now.

As 2 o'clock neared, the sound of many footsteps suddenly echoed on the stairs below. In seconds, a squad of 20 black men emerged at the top of the stairs just outside the courtroom where Minkins was being held. Dressed in the rain

DECLARATION of RESISTANCE

Many Northern communities, black and white, vowed to defy the detested Fugitive Slave Law. In October of 1850, African Americans meeting in Philadelphia adopted the following resolution.

DOCUMENT

Whereas, the Declaration of American Independence declares it to be a self-evident truth, "that all men are created equal, and are endowed by their Creator with certain inalienable rights, among which are life, liberty, and the pursuit of happiness"; and whereas, the Constitution of the United States, Art. 1, sect. 9, declares that "the privilege of the writ of habeas corpus shall not be suspended"; and in Art. 5 of the Amendments, that "no person shall be deprived of life, liberty, or property, without due process of law"; and whereas, the late Fugitive Slave Bill, recently enacted by the Congress of the United States, is in clear, palpable violation of these several provisions; therefore,

1. Resolved, That while we have heretofore yielded obedience to the laws of our country, however hard some of them have borne upon us, we deem this law so wicked, so atrocious, so utterly at variance with the principles of the Constitution; so subversive of the objects of all law, the protection of the lives, liberty, and property of the governed; so repugnant to the highest attributes of God, justice and mercy; and so horribly cruel in its clearly expressed mode of operation, that we deem it our sacred duty, a duty that we owe to ourselves, our wives, our children, and to our common nature, as well as to the panting fugitive from oppression, to resist this law at any cost and at all hazards; and we hereby pledge our lives, our fortunes, and our sacred honor so to do.

Paper Trails

On July 4, 2000, the *Hartford Courant* ran a startling front-page story recounting the paper's role in the slave trade during the 18th and 19th centuries. The story, titled "A Courant Complicity, An Old Wrong," detailed the *Courant*'s history of running ads — many signed by Thomas Green, the paper's founder — for the sale of slaves and the capture of runaways.

As the oldest continuously published newspaper in the U.S., the *Courant* felt compelled to apologize for its involvement: "We are not proud of that part of our history and apologize for any involvement by our predecessors at the *Courant* in the terrible practice of buying and selling human beings that took place in previous centuries."

The apology came on the heels of a *Courant* story from the previous March about the decision by Aetna, a Hartford-based insurance company, to apologize for having sold policies to slave owners insuring the lives of their slaves in the 1850s. Following that article, reporters conducted a four-month investigation of the newspaper's own archive and discovered that from its beginning in 1764 until well into the 19th century, "Courant publishers ... acted as slave brokers."

The *Courant* was not the first newspaper to acknowledge its involvement in the slave trade, nor will it likely be the last. In 1993, The New Orleans *Times-Picayune* revealed that it had run advertisements for slaves and runaways when it was known as the *Daily Picayune*. Following the *Courant* apology, other newspapers were reportedly preparing similar articles. Historians and civil rights activists expressed hope that news organizations would not only apologize for past actions but also acknowledge more recent failings and be able to speak more clearly to their readers about the complex issue of race.

---

gear of sailors, with sou'wester hats pulled down low to conceal their faces, they rushed to the courtroom door and wrenched it from the grip of the guards. "Hurt no one," one of the men cautioned as they surged in.

At the defense table, Minkins was startled by the commotion. He had not been forewarned of a rescue attempt. Who were these men rushing toward him? Would the officers open fire? Would they all be killed?

In an instant, the party of men raced to where Minkins stood, seized him and then retreated out the way they had come in, half-carrying the stunned fugitive. The feet of the men thundered on the stairs more loudly than before. When the rescuers emerged from the Court House doors with Minkins, loud cheering broke out. The rescue party hastily crossed Court Square, the curious following them like the tail of a comet. A woman in the crowd reached out to touch Minkins' hair and shouted, "God bless you!" as the fugitive was whisked away through the city streets.

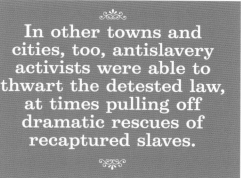

In other towns and cities, too, antislavery activists were able to thwart the detested law, at times pulling off dramatic rescues of recaptured slaves.

Minutes later the black "League of Freedom" escort — with Lewis Hayden at its head — entered the narrow streets of the African-American neighborhood on the back side of Beacon Hill. They soon vanished into the neighborhood's narrow alleyways, the clamorous rescue party evaporating as silently as raindrops after a summer shower.

Much later, Hayden revealed that he had secreted Minkins in the attic of Elizabeth Riley, widow of one of Boston's most successful African-American businessmen. Then, a few hours later, he had led Minkins to a safer location just outside Boston. That night, under the cover of darkness, Hayden and another "League of Freedom" member drove the rescued fugitive in a wagon 15 miles to the village of Concord, Massachusetts.

After Shadrach had eaten and rested for a few hours at the home of Ann and Francis Bigelow, two of Concord's many antislavery friends, he was sent on the Underground Railroad toward sanctuary in Canada. A week later, cold and weary but finally

Henry "Box" Brown acquired his nickname in 1850 by shipping himself to freedom in a wooden crate.

safe, Minkins arrived in Montreal, where he would live out his days as a free man.

For Boston's African Americans and their white allies, the rescue of Shadrach Minkins was cause for great rejoicing. They had succeeded in making a bold statement against an unjust law that supported an inhuman institution. But Lewis Hayden knew their victory was incomplete. More difficult challenges still lay ahead.

Supporters of the Fugitive Slave Law grew more determined than ever to force Boston to hand over a fugitive slave. Eventually, with a virtual army of guards and at great expense, Boston's federal officials succeeded in extracting two fugitive slaves from the city: Thomas Sims in 1851 and Anthony Burns in 1854. In both cases, rescue attempts had failed. After Sims was returned to slavery, Hayden felt compelled to send his wife, a fugitive herself, briefly into hiding in the countryside.

Yet the spectacle of watching Thomas Sims and Anthony Burns being marched back into slavery through the public streets of freedom-touting Boston shamed even those citizens who sympathized with the South. Slaveholders made only a few more token efforts to reclaim their human property in Boston, none of them successful. The black community safely hid dozens of threatened fugitive slaves or helped to spirit them out of the city. In other towns and cities, too — Cincinnati, Syracuse, Detroit, Milwaukee and many more — antislavery activists were able to thwart the detested law, at times pulling off dramatic rescues of recaptured slaves.

The fight in Boston and other locations to secure the freedom of their fugitive slaves helped focus the nation's attention on the gaping chasm between American ideals of freedom and the actualities of U.S. law that turned men, women and children into chattel. It announced that the time had come for the nation to face the appalling contradiction written into the Constitution.

It would take a bloody war to settle the issue of freedom once and for all. In 1865, the 13th Amendment finally accomplished what black and white abolitionists had been working toward for 200 years: the end of slavery. Never again would African Americans have to ask the question fugitive slave Shadrach Minkins demanded of his captors: "Who claims me?"

They claimed themselves. ⊠

Rebel With a Cause

The Religious Society of Friends, called Quakers, were among the first whites to denounce slavery in the colonies. But even this religious group, known for its egalitarian principles, sometimes wavered in its commitment to the cause of abolition. Slavery may have been a blight on man's soul, but it was also a profitable economic reality.

In 1737, a renegade congregant named Benjamin Lay began an all-out assault on the practice of slavery and the Quaker establishment that allowed it to continue. He published a 278-page tract entitled *All Slave-Keepers, that Keep the Innocent in Bondage.* In it, Lay condemned the Quaker civic and religious leadership of Pennsylvania, where he lived, for actions contrary to the tenets of the Society of Friends and to the dignity of life in general. Benjamin Franklin edited and printed *All Slave-Keepers* for Lay, but he did so anonymously; apart from its incendiary comments, publishing anti-slavery literature was illegal.

The Society leaders were furious. Slavery, though despicable, was good business. Furthermore, someone they viewed as a crazed upstart was questioning and disturbing the careful order of things. But Lay wasn't afraid of creating a disturbance to get people's attention. And he created many disturbances.

On one occasion, upon entering the Yearly Meeting of the Philadelphia Society of Friends, Lay threw off his cloak to reveal military regalia. In the stunned silence, he then produced a sword and stabbed through the Bible he was holding. Blood spurted from the Bible and splattered those Friends nearby who were already frozen in shock.

Standing before his Quaker brethren, Lay proclaimed, "Thus shall God shed the blood of those who have enslaved their fellow creatures!" The "blood" was actually berry juice which Lay had put in a sack and placed in the hollowed-out Bible. But whether blood or juice, the impact was what Lay was after.

On another occasion, Lay stood barefoot in the snow outside the meetinghouse. When Friends expressed concern that he was risking his health, Lay berated them for their hypocrisy: How could they offer him compassion yet ignore the more urgent needs of the ill-clad slaves who labored in their fields all winter? Another time, Lay "kidnapped" — and later returned — a child to show the boy's slaveholding parents what it felt like to have a loved one stolen away.

Benjamin Lay

IN CONTEXT ★ ★ ★

Lay's abolitionist feelings were hardly unique; many Friends agreed with him in principle, although they didn't share his combative style. In 1758, the Philadelphia Yearly Meeting granted authority to the monthly meetings to discipline any Friends who bought, sold or imported slaves into the colony. In response to this, Lay commented, "I can now die in peace," which he did, early the following year.

In 1790, nearly three decades after Lay's death, the Society of Friends sent the first petition to Congress condemning slavery as a moral evil and calling for the emancipation of all slaves. The rest of the country, however, would take longer to reach enlightenment; that it eventually did is due in no small part to the tireless efforts of abolitionists like Benjamin Lay, an unquiet man who had the ferocious courage of his convictions. He was, in his own words, "[a] poor common Sailor and an illiterate Man" who did what he did as "a General Service, by him that truly and sincerely desires the present and eternal Welfare and Happiness of all Mankind, all the World over, of all Colours, and Nations, as his own Soul."

3

Louisville, Kentucky ✣ 1870

Freedom's
MAIN LINE

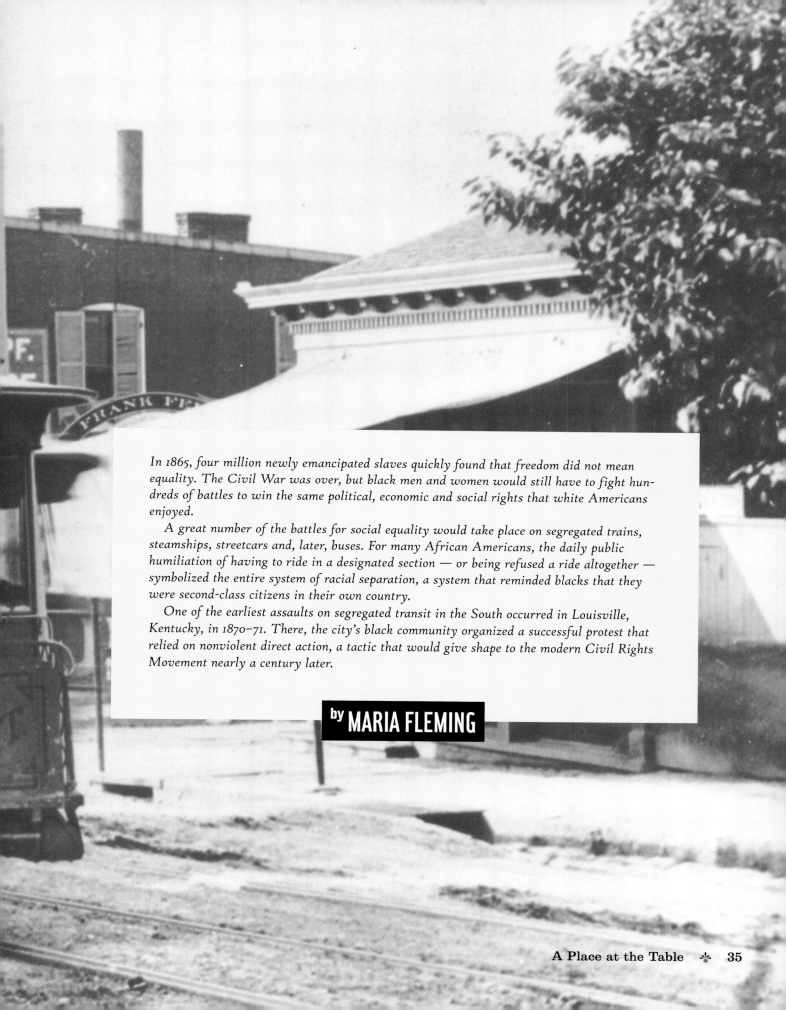

In 1865, four million newly emancipated slaves quickly found that freedom did not mean equality. The Civil War was over, but black men and women would still have to fight hundreds of battles to win the same political, economic and social rights that white Americans enjoyed.

A great number of the battles for social equality would take place on segregated trains, steamships, streetcars and, later, buses. For many African Americans, the daily public humiliation of having to ride in a designated section — or being refused a ride altogether — symbolized the entire system of racial separation, a system that reminded blacks that they were second-class citizens in their own country.

One of the earliest assaults on segregated transit in the South occurred in Louisville, Kentucky, in 1870–71. There, the city's black community organized a successful protest that relied on nonviolent direct action, a tactic that would give shape to the modern Civil Rights Movement nearly a century later.

by MARIA FLEMING

On October 30, 1870, three men outside Quinn Chapel in Louisville, Kentucky, made their way toward the trolley stand at Tenth and Walnut on the Central Passenger line. When the trolley stopped, each climbed aboard the near-empty car, dropped a coin in the fare box and took a seat. It would have been a routine occurrence — three men catching a ride home after church on a Sunday afternoon — had the passengers been white residents of Louisville. But they were African American. And for black city dwellers, riding a trolley was no ordinary act. It was a challenge to the entire social order.

As soon as the men entered the trolley car, a white passenger named John Russell told them to get off. The driver, too, demanded that they leave. Robert Fox, an elderly mortician, quietly replied that he and his companions — his brother Samuel, who was also his business partner, and Horace Pearce, who worked for both brothers — had the same right to ride as whites.

In fact, the trio's actions that day had been pre-arranged by Louisville's black community to test the legality of the streetcar companies' segregation policies. Under the policies, black women were allowed to ride the trolleys but on some lines they were forced to take seats in the rear of the car. Black men were usually permitted to ride only on the small front platform with the driver, and on some lines they couldn't ride at all.

Nearly 300 African-American men and women had gathered in front of Quinn Chapel that afternoon to show their support for what they hoped would lead to a legal decision striking down segregation on public carriers. Now a hush fell over the crowd as they waited to see what would happen.

The driver wasn't about to argue the question of black citizens' rights with Robert Fox. Nor was he going to proceed on his route. He sent a message to the streetcar company's central office that trouble was brewing and called out to other trolley drivers for assistance. Before long, a cluster of white drivers surrounded the three black men and began kicking them and shouting racial slurs. Then they dragged them off the trolley into the street.

The rough treatment of the men awakened the crowd in front of the chapel from its silence. Some

(*Above*) Louisville's trolley lines were the setting for one of the South's earliest protests against segregated transportation. (*Right*) The Brotherhood of Sleeping Car Porters, organized in 1925, was the first successful black trade union.

men grabbed chunks of hardened mud and began hurling them at the trolley car and yelling threats at the drivers. In the midst of the commotion, Pearce and the Fox brothers climbed back onto the car. They remained calm and composed, but now the men clenched stones in their fists. If the drivers attacked them again, they were ready to fight back.

The crowd shouted its support: "We'll pay your fines!" "We'll see you through this!" "Don't budge a step!" The superintendent of the Central Passenger Company came running up to the car. He said he'd return the men's fares if they got off the trolley immediately. Still, they refused.

By now, five trolleys had backed up on the tracks behind the halted car. The crowd seemed ready to erupt in violence just as three police officers arrived on the scene. The officers quickly arrested the three men for disorderly conduct and hauled them off to jail.

The streetcar protest in Louisville occurred during a time of tremendous upheaval in the South. The Civil War had ended just five years earlier. A period of Reconstruction was now underway as the federal government attempted to rebuild the former Confederate states economically, politically and socially and rejoin them to the Union.

Although it had been a slave state, Kentucky had remained loyal to the Union during the war. As a result, it was not subject to the federal Reconstruction policies that sought to reshape Southern state

governments and improve the status of the newly freed slaves. However, like the ex-Confederate states, Kentucky had also been transformed by the war and emancipation.

Before the Civil War, there had been no state-enforced separation of blacks and whites in public places in the South. From white Southerners' perspective, there had been no need. The institution of slavery clearly placed blacks at the bottom rung of society and established white supremacy. But following the war, Congress passed three new amendments to the Constitution abolishing slavery, extending citizenship rights to African Amerians, giving black men the right to vote and guaranteeing all African Americans equal protection under the law.

The old Southern social order, built on the bedrock of slavery, had suddenly crumbled. Many whites panicked. They could not envision a society where former slaves had the same rights they did.

Southern legislatures quickly introduced laws, known as Black Codes, that set limits on African Americans' freedom. Under these codes, which varied from state to state, blacks couldn't own or rent farmland; they could be imprisoned for assembling in public, using insulting language or not having a job; and they could be whipped by white employers.

BE DISSATISFIED

In the tumultuous years following the Civil War, scores of black leaders encouraged their communities to seize their rights. Speaking before a group of black college students in Nashville, Tennessee, in 1895, educator John Hope urged them to accept nothing less than full equality.

If we are not striving for equality, in heaven's name for what are we living? I regard it as cowardly and dishonest for any of our colored men to tell white people or colored people that we are not struggling for equality. ... Yes, my friends, I want equality. Nothing less. ... Now catch your breath, for I am going to use an adjective: I am going to say we demand social equality. ... I am no wild beast, nor am I an unclean thing.

Rise, Brothers! Come let us possess this land. ... Be discontented. Be dissatisfied. ... Be as restless as the tempestuous billows on the boundless sea. Let your discontent break mountain-high against the wall of prejudice, and swamp it to the very foundation.

FIRST PERSON

EAST LOUISIANA RAILROAD CO.

EXCURSIONS $1.00. | —TO THE— **GREAT ABITA SPRINGS.** | **E. S. FERGUSON,** G. P. A.

Some states and cities enacted statutes that called for segregated public transit, which until then had been a practice common only in Northern states. As one Mississippi newspaper declared, "We must keep the ex-slave in a position of inferiority. We must pass such laws as will make him *feel* his inferiority."

Another formidable obstacle stood in the path of blacks seeking political and social equality: the Ku Klux Klan. Ex-Confederate soldiers and planters formed the Klan in 1865. The secret terrorist organization tried to drive blacks — and whites sympathetic to their cause — away from the polls and thus keep them out of public office. The Klan also sought to keep blacks "in their place" socially. Newspapers throughout the South carried accounts of racial violence almost daily.

And yet, despite the political turmoil and ever-present threat of violence, Reconstruction was a period of tremendous hope and possibility for the newly emancipated slaves as well as free men and

Thirty-year-old Homer Plessy was jailed in 1892 for sitting in the "white" car of this train. In its landmark case *Plessy* v. *Ferguson*, the U.S. Supreme Court ruled that separate facilities were legal as long as they were "equal."

women of color. For two centuries, they had been struggling to break the chains of slavery and stand on equal footing with white Americans. Slavery was finally dead, and the federal government had acknowledged African Americans' civil and political rights. Now they were determined to exercise those rights.

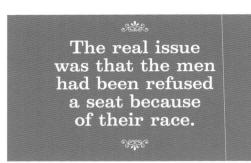

The real issue was that the men had been refused a seat because of their race.

The Fox brothers and Horace Pearce arrived in court the day after their arrest, prepared to make a case that they were entitled to the same treatment on the streetcars as white passengers. Col. John H. Ward, a white lawyer, defended the men. He pointed out that they had, in fact, been "exceedingly well behaved" during the incident, and thus the charge of disorderly conduct was not valid. The real issue, he said, was that the men had been refused a seat because of their race.

The Right to Ride

Segregated transportation was not limited to the Southern states. In fact, some historians trace the first use of the term "Jim Crow" to segregated railroad cars in the North. There, as in the South, blacks asserted their right to ride with whites. In 1854 — a century before Rosa Parks's now-famous act of civil disobedience — Elizabeth Jennings was forcibly removed from a segregated trolley car in New York City. Outraged by her mistreatment, Jennings sued the streetcar company. Her legal victory, along with further pressure from New York's African-American community, helped end segregation on the city's public transportation system. Following is Jennings's account of the incident that prompted her to file the suit.

Elizabeth Jennings Graham

Sarah E. Adams and myself walked down to the corner of Pearl and Chatham Sts. to take the Third Ave. cars. I held up my hand to the driver and he stopped the cars, we got on the platform, when the conductor told us to wait for the next car; I told him I could not wait, as I was in a hurry to go to church. . . . He then told me that the other car had my people in it, that it was appropriated for that purpose. I then told him I had no people. It was no particular occasion; I wished to go to church, as I had been going for the last six months, and I did not wish to be detained.

He insisted upon my getting off the car . . . but I did not get off the car. . . . He then said I should come out and he would put me out. I told him not to lay his hands on me; he took hold of me and I took hold of the window sash and held on; he pulled me until he broke my grasp and I took hold of his coat and held on to that, he also broke my grasp from that (but previously he had dragged my companion out, she all the while screaming for him to let go). He then ordered the driver to fasten his horses, which he did, and come and help him put me out of the car; they then both seized hold of me by the arms and pulled and dragged me flat down on the bottom of the platform, so that my feet hung one way and my head the other, nearly on the ground.

I screamed murder with all my voice, and my companion screamed out "you'll kill her; don't kill her."

The driver then let go of me and went to his horses; I went again in the car, and the conductor said you shall sweat for this; then told the driver to drive as fast as he could and not take another passenger in the car; to drive until he saw an officer or a Station House. They got an officer on the corner of Walker and Bowery, whom the conductor told that his orders from the agent were to admit colored persons if the passengers did not object, but if they did, not to let them ride. When the officer took me there were some eight or ten persons in the car. Then the officer, without listening to anything I had to say, thrust me out, and then pushed me, and tauntingly told me to get redress if I could.

"It is a small matter to assess a fine of from five to twenty dollars for disorderly conduct," Ward argued, "and that to us is no great thing; but it is a great thing for us to know whether or not we are to be debarred from all protection from injustice and wrong. They are good citizens . . . and they ask for simple justice and nothing more."

The judge, however, refused to consider the broader issue that Ward raised. He ruled only that the men had indeed created a disturbance and fined them $5.

Louisville's black community, however, was not about to let the more pressing question of their rights go unanswered. Backed by the city's African-American leaders, Robert Fox decided to sue the Central Passenger Railroad Company for denying him access to its streetcars.

Because the state courts did not allow black testimony, Fox filed his suit the following week in the

U.S. district court in Louisville. During the winter, many African Americans boycotted city streetcars as they waited for the federal court to hand down its decision.

On May 11, 1871, the district court ruled on behalf of Fox. The monetary award was small — $15 — but it represented a huge symbolic victory for Louisville's black community. Triumphant, black men and women immediately began to test their right to ride. However, they soon found that the court was far more willing to recognize their status as equal citizens than Louisville's white residents.

The day of the ruling, a black man boarded a car on Jefferson Street. When the driver demanded he get off, the man refused to move. The operator drove the car off the tracks. He, too, refused to move. For half an hour, the two men sat in silence. Outside, tension mounted as a crowd of blacks and

FIRST PERSON UNITE and CONQUER

In all of their civil rights struggles, black Americans received support from white allies. Jewish Americans could often be counted on to stand with African Americans in the cause of justice. Jews were involved in the creation of the National Association for the Advancement of Colored People and the National Urban League. They also participated in large numbers in the Civil Rights Movement of 1954–65.

Martin Luther King Jr. pointed out that blacks and Jews shared both a common history of oppression and a common fight against the enemies of democracy. "[O]ur glory," King said, "is that we are chosen to prove that courage is a characteristic of oppressed people, however cynically and brutally they are denied full equality and freedom."

In the weeks leading up to the 1963 March on Washington — where King would deliver his historic "I Have a Dream" speech to a crowd of 250,000 — the American Jewish Committee declared its support for the cause of black civil rights and for the demonstration.

[The] pledge of first-class citizenship and freedom for the American Negro remains tragically unfulfilled. This enor-

mous gap between promise and actuality underscores the justifiable impatience with which Negroes are insistently demanding their full democratic rights now. As members of a group . . . which has from time immemorial known oppression and felt the indignities of discrimination, Jews understand the frustrations experienced by our Negro fellow citizens. We share with them the determination to eliminate swiftly the injustices from which they suffer.

The . . . March on Washington . . . will demonstrate the deep commitment of a vast majority of the American people to the attainment of full equality for all. . . . We believe the March to be in the greatest tradition of peaceable assembly for a redress of grievances and therefore vigorously support local affiliates throughout the nation who desire to participate in this historic event.

The Jews have always been part of the eternal quest for human dignity and social justice for all mankind. Our devotion to this cause is rooted deeply in our religious and spiritual traditions and our social experience. A most appropriate means of expressing our ideals today, as Americans and Jews, consists in joining together with all men of good will in this peaceful and lawful assembly for the realization of a more humane and democratic society.

whites began to gather around the car. Finally, the black passenger stepped off the trolley, and the crowd dispersed. But the demonstrator had established a pattern for other "ride-ins" that would soon follow.

During the next three days, black citizens boarded streetcars throughout the city. When they would not get off, drivers ran the trolleys off the tracks, refusing to proceed on their routes. Soon, cars began to back up on the trolley lines, clogging the streets and wreaking havoc on the city's public transportation system.

Several times, the trolley operator and white passengers abandoned the streetcars when protesters wouldn't leave. Black riders didn't waste any time taking the operators' places and driving the streetcars themselves. Sometimes, the protesters were spotted with their feet up on the cushioned seats, smoking cigars as they cruised along the tracks, and a throng of black supporters cheered them on.

City and state officials denounced the court's ruling and refused to enforce it. Louisville's three newspapers rebuked the protesters for stirring up trouble in an otherwise tranquil city. Their editors promoted the idea of separate cars for black riders as a way to restore peace. The African-American community immediately rejected the suggestion.

Black passengers were committed to using nonviolent resistance during the protest. Those participating in the "ride-ins" maintained a steely composure in the face of hostile white mobs and rough treatment. Sometimes drivers and white passengers tried to forcibly eject the demonstrators, grabbing them by their feet and dragging them from the cars.

On one streetcar line, a group of white riders threw a black passenger out a window. Another time, a group of white newsboys beat a black man attempting to board a car. Everywhere, black and white onlookers clustered on street corners and spilled into the streets, watching and waiting.

On Friday, May 12, the demonstration reached a climax, with protesters staging "ride-ins" on every streetcar line in the city. As dusk fell, an angry white crowd gathered in front of the Willard Hotel. There, a black teenager named Carey Duncan quietly climbed onto a trolley. Duncan sat impas-

Jim Crow laws segregating railway passengers were common across the U.S. in the 19th century.

> Black passengers were committed to using nonviolent resistance during the protest.

sively as he watched the mob swarm around the streetcar. Suddenly, they began to rock the car, trying to overturn it. Duncan grabbed hold of the seat and hung on for his life. The crowd roared: "Put him out!" "Hit him!" "Kick him!" "Hang him!"

On the sidewalk in front of the hotel stood Louisville's chief of police. He watched as a gang of white teenagers climbed aboard the car and threatened Duncan, shouting insults in his face. Still, Duncan didn't move or make a sound. He stared straight ahead. The gang dragged Duncan from the car and began to beat him. Finally, Duncan's resolve to remain impassive broke down, and he fought back.

By now, black men and women had gathered in the street, too, and the police feared the mass of people was about to explode in violence. Several officers stepped in and grabbed Duncan and quickly broke up the crowd. Duncan was later charged with disorderly conduct. The youths who beat him went free.

Rosa Parks's act of civil disobedience in December 1955 expressed the feelings of thousands of others toward Jim Crow restrictions.

After two days of clashes on city streets, the community's nerves were frayed. Everywhere, tempers ran high, and a full-scale race riot threatened. Rumors spread that the federal government was sending troops to restore order. Louisville's mayor quickly arranged for people on both sides of the controversy to meet.

On Saturday, May 13, Mayor John George Baxter Jr. sat down with leaders in the black community and their lawyers, representatives from streetcar companies and the chief of police to negotiate a settlement. The companies' owners had grown nervous that prolonging the battle over their segregation policies would hurt profits. They also recognized

Get on the Bus

In 1961, interracial groups of civil rights activists organized a series of "Freedom Rides" to protest segregation on interstate buses and in bus stations. Segregation had already been declared unconstitutional by the Supreme Court, but the court's rulings were not being enforced.

Like the black men and women who had staged "ride-ins" on Louisville's streetcars nearly a century before, the Freedom Riders planned to test their court-recognized rights for integrated travel. White protesters would sit in the back of the bus while black passengers took seats in the front. At bus terminals, both blacks and whites would use seating areas, restrooms and other facilities without regard to racial restrictions.

On May 4, 1961, the first group of Freedom Riders set out from Washington, D.C., on what was to be a two-week journey through the heart of the South. But their trip came to an abrupt halt 10 days later at a rest stop in Anniston, Alabama, where a mob of 200 whites attacked the protesters and set their bus on fire.

A second bus carrying Freedom Riders faced a similar fate later that day in Birmingham, Alabama. There, another mob savagely beat demonstrators.

Despite the violence, more Freedom Rides followed, and by summer's end the protesters had achieved their goal. The Interstate Commerce Commission issued regulations enforcing integration on interstate buses and in terminals.

Freedom Riders attempting to integrate interstate bus lines in the South met with violence in Alabama.

During the Mongomery (Alabama) Bus Boycott of 1955–56, protesters walked or arranged car pools to avoid riding city buses.

that — given the current political climate in the South, with the federal government stepping forward to advance and protect blacks' rights — this was a fight that ultimately they couldn't win.

They agreed to give in to the protesters' demands. After a long struggle, Louisville's African-American citizens had finally attained "simple justice": the right to ride the city's streetcars without restriction.

Louisville's African-American community was jubilant. But in the decades to come, there would be many more battles to fight, in Kentucky and throughout the South. In 1877, Reconstruction — and the promise of change it offered blacks — came to an end. The federal government's attention drifted away from the South and the nation's racial problems.

New laws established by the South's "redeemer" governments sought to fully restore white power and supremacy

Life and Death Struggle

For nearly three centuries, custom dictated that blacks and whites in both Northern and Southern states be interred in separate cemeteries. As one observer in Alabama noted, "If a colored person was to be buried among the whites, the latter would all rise from their graves in indignation."

Thaddeus Stevens, a white U.S. Congressman from Pennsylvania, devoted his life to fighting slavery and all forms of racial oppression, including segregation. Before his death in 1868, he chose a burial site in Lancaster, Pennsylvania, in a small, remote cemetery that did not subscribe to the dictates of segregation. He made arrangements that his tombstone bear the following inscription so that he might continue to spread the message of racial justice, even after his death:

I repose in this quiet and secluded spot
Not from any natural preference for solitude
But, finding other Cemeteries limited as to
    Race by Charter Rules,
I have chosen this that I might illustrate in my death
The Principles which I advocated
Through a long life
EQUALITY OF MAN BEFORE HIS CREATOR.

DOCUMENT

After more than a year of sustained effort, the Montgomery Bus Boycott finally broke the color barrier on the city's buses.

and eroded many of the advances blacks had made during the Reconstruction era. By 1890, the Black Codes had solidified into the system of racial separation and discrimination known as Jim Crow.

This system was given full legal sanction in 1896 through the U.S. Supreme Court ruling in *Plessy* v. *Ferguson*, which said that the 14th Amendment was not intended to enforce social equality between the races.

The decision would not be reversed until 1954. In the meantime, Jim Crow was free to flourish in the South, not just on streetcars, but in schools, libraries, parks, hotels, theaters and other public facilities.

African Americans never ceased pressing for their rights, however. When a series of new laws were enacted in Southern cities and states establishing segregation on streetcars in the early 1900s, a wave of protest swept through the region. Black men and women held rallies, organized petition drives and planned legal attacks on the new laws. Between 1900 and 1906, in more than 25 Southern cities, they boycotted transit companies to protest segregated streetcars.

The boycotts lasted from several months to several years. In many cities, blacks established their own informal transit systems during the protests by enlisting the services of private carriages, hacks (horse-drawn "taxis") and drays (carts and wagons used to haul goods). In Houston, Texas, when a streetcar strike left whites without transportation in 1904, African-American draymen took pleasure in roping off the rear section of their carts and posting signs that read "For Whites Only."

Most of the boycotts failed, however. A few brought short-lived victories, but, in each case, Jim Crow measures were eventually reinstated.

Only in Louisville were African Americans successful in keeping Jim Crow off city streetcars. There, too, whites repeatedly tried to resegregate the trolleys. But Louisville's black citizens fought the Jim Crow ordinances every time they were proposed and held onto their hard-won right to ride — even as segregation increasingly defined other aspects of city life.

Although African Americans throughout the South never stopped fighting segregation, it would take another half-century before they were able to stamp out Jim Crow. In 1955, a civil rights activist named Rosa Parks, backed by a community of reformers in Montgomery, Alabama, would stage a one-woman "ride-in" of her own. She ignited a civil rights revolution — in the making since the end of the Civil War — that would pull down the walls of segregation once and for all. ⊠

A Second Revolution

Some historians have called the period of Reconstruction that followed the Civil War the "second American Revolution" and the 13th, 14th and 15th Amendments a "second Bill of Rights" for African Americans. The aim of Reconstruction and these amendments was to free black Americans from white oppression and to give them full citizenship rights in the country they had helped build.

This second revolution would ultimately fail, however, although the scholar and civil rights activist W. E. B. Du Bois would call it "a glorious failure." Reconstruction's glory rested in the fact that the rights of African Americans were finally written into the Constitution of the United States. However, these rights largely remained promises on paper only.

The 14th Amendment, ratified in 1868, guaranteed blacks "equal protection of the laws." But states routinely disregarded the amendment's "equal protection" provision. The Supreme Court itself stripped the law of impact when it ruled in *Plessy* v. *Ferguson* in 1896 that segregated facilities were not by nature unequal, and the system of Jim Crow segregation flourished in the South.

Voting rights were guaranteed to blacks under the 15th Amendment, ratified in 1870, which said that citizens could not be denied the vote on the basis of "race, color, or previous condition of servitude." But states found ways around this law, too, instituting poll taxes, literacy tests and grandfather clauses (which stipulated that a man could vote only if his father or grandfather had voted). All of these measures were designed to prevent black men from voting. But because the language of the state laws did not explicitly target African Americans, the courts upheld them. Violence and intimidation were also used to keep blacks away from the polls and thus shut them out of the political process.

African Americans' efforts to secure their rights did not die with the unfulfilled promises of Reconstruction, however. Black men and women and their white allies continued to organize and agitate for change, voicing their demand for racial justice in the black press and forming civil rights organizations of local and national scope, including the Niagara Movement in 1905, the National Association for the Advancement of Colored People (NAACP) in 1909, and the National Urban League in 1911.

AT ISSUE
★ ★ ★

The diverse and persistent efforts of many individuals and groups would coalesce in the modern Civil Rights Movement of 1954–65. During this period, widespread legal action, sit-ins, marches and other nonviolent protests pressured the courts and federal government to enforce the guarantees of the Reconstruction amendments. In fact, some historians have called the Civil Rights Movement the "second Reconstruction" because it finally realized the promises made to black Americans after the Civil War.

In 1954, the U.S. Supreme Court nullified the doctrine of "separate but equal" in its landmark *Brown* v. *Board of Education* ruling, restoring the power of the 14th Amendment's equal protection clause. A decade later, Congress passed the Civil Rights Act of 1964, which made it illegal to discriminate against blacks in employment and accommodations and put the last nails in the coffin of Jim Crow. In 1965, the Voting Rights Act outlawed poll taxes, literacy tests and other discriminatory practices, finally allowing African Americans to fully exercise the right to vote that the 15th Amendment had promised them nearly a century earlier.

The sweeping civil rights changes of the 1950s and '60s were the victories not only of celebrated heroes such as Rosa Parks and Martin Luther King Jr. but of the countless foot soldiers such as Robert Fox who fought the early battles of our nation's civil rights revolution.

THIS LAND is OURS

Native Americans' identities have always been closely linked to the land. Tecumseh, Osceola, Sitting Bull, Geronimo and Chief Joseph are just a few of the Native resistance leaders who fought to hold onto their ancestral homes and their cultures during the European American land grab of the 18th and 19th centuries. But outnumbered and outgunned, Native Americans stood little chance against the surging white population. Eventually, the U.S. govern-ment would seize two billion acres of their territories.

In the late 1800s, however, a small band of American Indians, determined to keep their homeland, brought their case to the federal courts. Their legal victory was the first to recognize Native rights to personal freedom and legal protection under the U.S. Constitution. The case would pave the way for other legal challenges to U.S. Indian policy in the decades that followed.

by BRANDON MARIE MILLER

A Place

On a biting cold day in February 1877, Chief Standing Bear's heart chilled with misgivings. He surveyed a land barren of trees, littered with rocks, the river dry. This land, labeled "Indian Territory," was where the United States government intended his people, the Ponca, to live. But it could never replace their home near the mouth of the Niobrara River on the High Plains, where the Ponca had farmed and hunted buffalo for almost 200 years.

Nineteen winters had passed since the Ponca had ceded thousands of acres to the government. In return, officials assured the Ponca they would keep their lands on the Niobrara, the "swift running water," as their permanent home. But, as always, the U.S. government wanted more.

Like other tribes, the Ponca watched the years pass while whites poured onto Native American lands, accompanied by soldiers, followed by the railroads. They destroyed the buffalo and other game the Plains people depended upon. The whites spread new diseases that killed thousands of Native Americans. And the Indian people forced onto government reservation lands often went hungry, dependent on food rationed by government agents.

Some Plains cultures like the Sioux, Cheyenne and Comanche fought for their homelands. But the Ponca were not a warrior people; resistance to an endless wave of well-supplied soldiers seemed to promise certain death.

Hoping to ensure their nation's survival, the Ponca welcomed a mission church and school on their reservation, in what is present-day Nebraska. They worked their fields with reapers and mowers and other farming tools used by white people. Many families abandoned earth lodges for the log houses of the settlers. By adopting white ways, and by not raising arms against U.S. soldiers or settlers, the Ponca sought leverage to hold the government to treaty promises and, more importantly, to keep their homelands.

But the government rewarded the Ponca's peaceful cooperation by disbursing only a trickle of the money and supplies promised in the 1858 treaty. Ten years later, in another treaty, the government mistakenly granted the Ponca's "permanent" homeland to the Sioux. Ponca cries for justice fell on deaf ears.

The last bitter stroke for Standing Bear's people came in January 1877, when U.S. Indian Inspector Edward Kemble arrived at the Ponca agency. The government had decided to remove the Ponca from the Niobrara to Indian Territory in what is now Oklahoma.

Stunned voices rose in protest. "This land is ours," Standing Bear objected. "We have never sold it. Here we wish to live and die. We have harmed no man. We have kept our treaty."

Kemble promised that no decision would be made until a delegation of chiefs looked over the new land. If the Ponca did not favor southern lands, they could speak to the "Great Father" — President Ulysses S. Grant — and stay along the Niobrara.

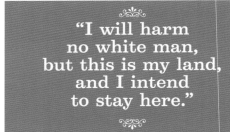

"I will harm no white man, but this is my land, and I intend to stay here."

Now, as they stood on those very lands and gazed across the bleak expanse before them, the Ponca chiefs shared their impressions in hushed voices. They asked to telegraph the Great Father and tell him they were not satisfied with the Indian Territory lands. Kemble's agreeable manner changed; he refused their request. The Ponca, he informed the chiefs, *would* be moved. When the chiefs said they only wanted to return north to their homeland, Kemble replied, "Walk there if you want to."

The delegation debated what to do. Chief White Eagle recalled, "We thought we should die, and [I] felt that I should cry, but I remembered that I was a man."

Kemble denied the chiefs any money or a pass they could show if stopped by whites. The February winds howled outside, scouring the plains of Kansas and Nebraska with snow. The Ponca, each wrapped in a blanket, began the 500-mile trek back to their home on the Niobrara. To survive, the men ate raw corn they found drying in fields. At night, they slept in haystacks to stay warm. Before long, the Ponca's moccasins wore out, and they trudged through the snow barefoot. Each step stiffened their determination to contest the government's demand that they move south.

Forty days later, starving and weak, the Ponca delegation arrived back in Nebraska, only to be met by Kemble, who had hurried there ahead of them. The government agent had already pressured about

Standing Bear and his wife had already lost two children when their oldest son died in the harsh conditions of the southern territory.

170 Ponca into relocating. The chiefs, including Standing Bear, protested. "I will harm no white man," he said, "but this is my land, and I intend to stay here." Kemble had the outspoken chief arrested and taken to Fort Randall, in Indian Territory near the Nebraska border.

Soon another government agent, E. A. Howard, arrived. As a gesture of goodwill, he released Standing Bear and settled in to convince the Ponca they had to move. But the chiefs stood firm. Finally, after a four-hour council meeting on May 15, Howard issued a weary ultimatum: "Will you go peaceably or by force?"

By adopting white ways, and by not raising arms against white settlers or soldiers, the Ponca sought leverage to keep their homelands.

The chiefs stared at Howard in stony silence. Then a boy ran up and cried, "The soldiers have come to the lodges!" The Ponca, it turned out, had never had a choice. Fighting was useless, and the chiefs sadly relented before the show of military power. "The soldiers came with their guns and bayonets," recalled Standing Bear, ". . . our people and our children were crying."

On May 16, 1877, blue-coated soldiers surrounded the village of 700 people. The soldiers drove the Ponca "as one would drive a herd of ponies" across the Niobrara. Howard kept a diary of the march south, a journey rife with suffering as the Ponca battled constant torrential rain, camped in mud, crossed swollen rivers, even endured a tornado. People broke down in cold, hunger and illness. Many died along the way. Among the dead were children weakened by exposure. Even so, Howard noted their fortitude and wrote more than once: "The Indians during the day behaved well, and marched splendidly."

A PLEA FOR FORGIVENESS

Beginning in colonial times, white Americans attempted to Christianize Indians, believing that Native forms of worship were primitive and barbaric. Although some Indians' conversion to Christianity was voluntary and genuine, Native adoption of the Christian religion was often coerced or used by the U.S. government as a bargaining tool: Those who embraced Christianity — such as the Ponca — were granted special benefits and protections. In 1987, Catholics, Baptists, Methodists, Presbyterians, Episcopalians and other Christian denominations in the Pacific Northwest issued an apology to the region's tribal councils for the part their churches played in the religious oppression of America's Native peoples.

DOCUMENT

Dear Brothers and Sisters,

This is a formal apology on behalf of our churches for their long-standing participation in the destruction of traditional Native American spiritual practices. We call upon our people for recognition of and respect for your traditional ways of life and for protection of your sacred places and ceremonial objects. We have frequently been unconscious and insensitive and have not come to your aid when you have been victimized by unjust Federal policies and practices. In many other circumstances we reflected the rampant racism and prejudice of the dominant culture with which we too willingly identified. During the 200th Anniversary year of the United States Constitution we, as leaders of our churches in the Pacific Northwest, extend our apology. We ask for your forgiveness and blessing. . . .

[W]e call upon the people of our denominations and fellowships to a commitment of mutual support in your efforts to reclaim and protect the legacy of your own traditional spiritual teachings.

On July 9, fighting swarms of biting flies, the Ponca reached their new home in Indian territory. "The people were all nearly worn out from the fatigue of the march," Howard wrote, "and were heartily glad that the long tedious journey was at an end, that they might . . . rest." They joined the first group of 170 Ponca removed earlier and now existing in a miserable camp of tents.

The government had provided no supplies, tools or food for the Ponca; their own farm tools and most of their belongings had been confiscated by the soldiers back in Nebraska.

"This was all different from our own home," Standing Bear later recalled. "There [in the north] we raised all we needed. Here there was no work to do. We had nothing to work with, and there was no man to hire us. . . . All my people were heart-broken. I was like a child. I could not help even myself, much less help them."

How were they to feed and clothe themselves? That first year, the adverse climate, poor nutrition and malaria left many sick and dying; some 158 people had died since they'd left the banks of the Niobrara. In July 1878, the government allowed the Ponca to trudge another 150 miles west to new lands along the Arkansas River. The land was better, but again, with few supplies it was hard to make a go of things.

Chief White Eagle recalled, "The land was good. But in summer we were sick again. We were as grass that is trodden down, we and our stock. Then came the cold weather, and how many died we did not know."

Standing Bear had already lost two children when his oldest son died. "He begged me to take him, when he was dead, back to our old burying ground," said the chief.

In January 1879, Standing Bear and about 30 others fled the reservation and headed north. They avoided settlements and eluded soldiers, arriving in March at the Nebraska reservation of their friends, the Omaha tribe. Gen. George Crook, stationed in Omaha as commander of the army's Department of the Platte, received orders to send soldiers to the Omaha reservation and arrest Standing Bear. As soon as possible, the renegade Ponca would be shipped back to Indian Territory in Oklahoma.

Gen. George Crook, as a good soldier, followed orders. But after years of fighting Native Americans, he'd come to admire and sympa-

thize with many of the tribes. More than once in official correspondence with the War Department, Crook voiced complaints over the government's inhumane treatment of Native Americans. This time, Crook contacted Thomas Henry Tibbles, an editor with the *Omaha Herald*. Was there a way to use the power of the press to aid the Ponca?

On March 31, 1879, Crook met with the imprisoned Ponca at the Fort Omaha guardhouse. For their interview, Standing Bear stood before Crook dressed as a leader of his people in the full regalia of a Ponca chief. "I thought God intended us to live," he addressed the General. "But I was mistaken. God

Gen. George Crook called the prospect of sending the Ponca back to the Indian Territory they had fled a "very disagreeable duty."

intends to give the country to the White people, and we are to die."

Standing Bear's eloquence and demeanor impressed Crook. The General promised he would try and wait until the Ponca and their horses had time to recover before taking them back to Indian Territory. "It is," said Crook, "a very disagreeable duty."

Meanwhile, Tibbles kept the telegraph wires sizzling with word of the Ponca's plight. Churches in Omaha pledged support. A young lawyer, John L. Webster, volunteered aid. He was soon joined by Andrew Poppleton, another Omaha lawyer.

The lawyers, working for free, rushed to find a way to prevent the removal of Standing Bear and his people back to Indian Territory. "The Indians have been held by the courts as 'wards of the nation,'" noted Poppleton, "but it does not follow ... [that] the guardian can imprison, starve, or practice inhumane cruelty upon the ward."

Webster and Poppleton gained the support of Judge Elmer S. Dundy, and, with Crook's compli-

Standing Bear (4th from left) and his fellow chiefs reminded federal agents that, unlike the U.S. government, the Ponca had never broken a treaty.

ance, the Judge issued a writ of *habeas corpus* against Crook. A writ of *habeas corpus* requires that a prisoner be brought before the court to decide the legality of his imprisonment. The General had to show by what authority he held the Ponca under arrest.

Crook presented the court with his military orders. U.S. District Attorney G. M. Lambertson appeared before Judge Dundy and denied the Ponca had any right to a writ of *habeas corpus* on the grounds that Indians were not citizens; they were not even "persons within the meaning of the law." Therefore, Standing Bear could not bring a case against the government. The judge elected to hear arguments, and the case of *Standing Bear* v. *Crook* began on April 30, 1879.

The trial lasted two days. Webster and Poppleton argued that in times of peace, no Native American could be forced from one place to another without

"Let Me Be a Free Man"

In 1877, Chief Joseph led a four-month battle against U.S. troops who tried to force his tribe, the Nez Percé, from their homeland in the Pacific Northwest's Wallowa Valley onto a reservation. The Nez Percé were ultimately overpowered and removed to Indian Territory, but Chief Joseph continued to fight for American Indian rights until his death in 1904. In 1879, he traveled to Washington, D.C., where he exhorted U.S. leaders to treat Indians more justly.

Words do not pay for my dead people. They do not pay for my country, now overrun by white men. They do not protect my father's grave. They do not pay for all my horses and cattle. Good words will not give me back my children. . . . Good words will not give my people good health and stop them from dying. Good words will not get my people a home where they can live in peace and take care of themselves. I am tired of talk that comes to nothing. . . . If the white man wants to live in peace with the Indian he can live in peace. There need be no trouble. Treat all men alike. Give them all the same

law. Give them all an even chance to live and grow. All men were made by the same Great Spirit Chief. They are all brothers. The earth is the mother of all people, and all people should have equal rights upon it. . . . I have asked some of the great white chiefs where they get their authority to say to the Indian that he shall stay in one place, while he sees white men going where they please. They cannot tell me.

I only ask of the government to be treated as all other men are treated. . . .

Let me be a free man — free to travel, free to stop, free to work, free to trade where I choose, free to choose my own teachers, free to follow the religion of my fathers, free to think and talk and act for myself — and I will obey every law, or submit to the penalty.

FIRST PERSON

his consent. More importantly, the lawyers asserted that Native Americans were indeed "persons" before the law. Under the Constitution, Standing Bear possessed some of the same rights and freedoms as white men.

Government lawyers, however, insisted that the Ponca had to live by rules the government established just for Indian nations.

Over Lambertson's objection, Judge Dundy granted Standing Bear permission to speak. All eyes were riveted on the Ponca chief as he described, through an interpreter, the ill treatment his people had received.

> The notion that Indians were people entitled to protection under the law reflected a growing change in public opinion.

With hands raised to the judge, Standing Bear made his case. "That hand," he said, "is not the color of yours, but if I pierce it, I shall feel pain. If you pierce your hand, you also feel pain. The blood that will flow from mine will be of the same color as yours. The same God made us both. . . . If a white man had land, and someone should swindle him, that man would try to get it back, and you would not blame him.

"Look on me," cried the chief. "Take pity on me, and help me to save the lives of the women and children. My brothers, a power, which I cannot resist, crowds me down to the ground. I need help." Many people wept at Standing Bear's words; the judge and General Crook were visibly moved.

Judge Dundy took several days to write his legal opinion. He then ruled that "an Indian is a person within the meaning of the laws of the United States" and could not be forcibly moved or confined to a reservation without his consent.

"The Poncas are amongst the most peaceable and friendly of all the Indians tribes," Judge Dundy wrote. "If they could be removed to the In[dian] Territory by force, and kept there in the same way, I can see no good reason why they might not be taken and kept by force in the penitentiary.... I cannot think that any such arbitrary authority exists in this country."

The Judge's decision brought the courtroom spectators cheering to their feet. The 60-year-old Ponca chief had gained recognition that Native Americans had rights of human dignity under the laws of the land. General Crook was the first to reach Standing Bear and shake his hand.

Standing Bear and his handful of Ponca followers were allowed to return to the Omaha reservation. Eventually, in another small victory, they were granted a slice of their old homelands to live upon. The rest of the Ponca living in Indian Territory were not permitted to return north. Standing Bear's hard-won return to his beloved Niobrara carried the cost of dividing his tribe.

Congress set up a commission, which included Crook, to further examine the Ponca's situation. The commission held hearings in Washington, D.C., and traveled to the Ponca reservation in Indian Territory, as well as to Standing Bear's small clan in Nebraska. Congress officially recognized that the Ponca had been moved "without authority or law" and appropriated funds as compensation.

Standing Bear's victory raised more questions than it answered.

The southern Ponca, under the leadership of Chief White Eagle, decided to avoid further turmoil and remain on the new lands. Fresh money and supplies had helped them build homes and schools and buy tools to start life anew. So the Ponca remained a divided people, with the majority living in Indian Territory and Standing Bear's small band of followers in Nebraska.

For its time, the trial of Standing Bear was a landmark court decision. The judge's ruling represented a huge symbolic victory for Native peoples. For centuries, whites had labeled Indians

A Crime Against the Country

Not every U.S. citizen endorsed the removal of Indians to reservations. Some supported Native efforts to hold onto lands that were rightfully theirs. In 1838, author Ralph Waldo Emerson wrote an open letter to U.S. President Martin Van Buren expressing his outrage at the not-yet-signed Indian Removal Act. Van Buren did sign the act into law, setting the stage for the infamous Cherokee Trail of Tears. Emerson wrote:

The soul of man, the justice, the mercy that is the heart's heart in all men, from Maine to Georgia, does abhor this business. . . . A crime is projected that confounds our understandings by its magnitude — a crime that really deprives us as well as the Cherokees of a country, for how could we call the conspiracy that should crush these poor Indians our government, or the land that was cursed by their parting and dying imprecations our country, any more? You, sir, will bring down that renowned chair in which you sit into infamy if your seal is set to this instrument of perfidy; and the name of this nation, hitherto the sweet omen of religion and liberty, will stink to the world.

Reclaiming Lost Lands

In 1890, a Sioux elder described the history of U.S. government dealings with the Indians this way: "They made us many promises, more than I can remember, but they never kept but one; they promised to take our land and they took it."

Indeed, since the arrival of European colonists, Native peoples' land base has shrunk from 2 billion acres to 56 million acres — barely 2 percent of the United States. In recent decades, however, Native Americans have waged successful battles in the courts to reclaim some of their lost lands.

☞ For thousands of years, Blue Lake, in present-day New Mexico, has been the Taos Pueblo's holiest shrine. In 1906, the U.S. government adjoined the lake, without the Taos peoples' consent, to the Carson National Forest. For the next 65 years, the Taos Pueblo tirelessly lobbied Congress and appealed to the American public for the return of this sacred site. Finally, in 1972, the U.S. government restored Blue Lake and 48,000 acres of land surrounding it to the Taos people.

☞ In 1971, Alaska's Native peoples won the largest land settlement in American history, attaining federal recognition of their title to 44 million acres of the state. In addition, they were awarded $962.5 million as compensation for other lands that they lost when Alaska was made a state in 1959.

☞ In 1980, the Passamaquoddy and Penobscot tribes were able to prove that they held legal title to nearly two-thirds of the state of Maine. The tribes accepted a multi-million dollar settlement and the return of 300,000 acres of land.

☞ In the longest unresolved Indian land claim in the country, the Lakota — also known as the Western Sioux, a name now considered derogatory — have demanded the return of their sacred Black Hills in South Dakota. Under treaties made in 1851 and 1868, the Lakota were guaranteed title to the Black Hills, but the government opened the land to white settlement when gold was discovered in the area. This led to military conflicts with the United States, including the famous 1876 Battle of the Little Bighorn.

Ultimately, the U.S. government ceded the lands, and the Lakota have fought for more than a century to get them back. In 1980, the U.S. Supreme Court recognized the Lakota claim to the Black Hills and awarded the tribes $105 million as compensation for the land they lost. But the Lakota — who live in the poorest county in the U.S. — rejected the cash settlement. Today they continue to fight for the return of the Black Hills, which they consider central to their cultural and spiritual identity.

"savages" and used a belief in Native inferiority to justify broken treaties, land theft, even mass murder. The notion that Indians were people entitled to protection under the law reflected a growing change in public opinion.

However, Standing Bear's victory actually raised more questions than it answered. How would Native interests be represented and protected within the U.S. political system? Many white people, including Chief Standing Bear's supporters, hoped for Indian policy reform. Yet most whites believed the only way Indians could survive was to adopt white ways.

During the court case, Standing Bear's lawyers tried to show that the Ponca were attempting to live within the white definition of "civilized": They had built homes, sent their children to schools; many had become Christians. Therefore, the Ponca deserved the same protection as U.S. citizens.

White recognition of Indian "personhood," it seemed, came with a condition: Give up your culture and become like us.

In addition, Judge Dundy did not question the authority of the United States over Native American nations. While his decision suggested that Native peoples had the same rights to personal freedom and legal protection as U.S. citizens, it did not acknowledge that Indian tribes had any rights to self-government.

In time, American Indians themselves raised these issues as they continued the struggle to preserve their lands and cultures. The Ponca's challenge of the U.S. government marked a turning point on the long path of Indian resistance. Increasingly, after *Standing Bear* v. *Crook*, the fight for Native rights would shift from the battlefields to the courtrooms of the growing nation. ◘

THE STRIKE
FOR
THREE LOAVES

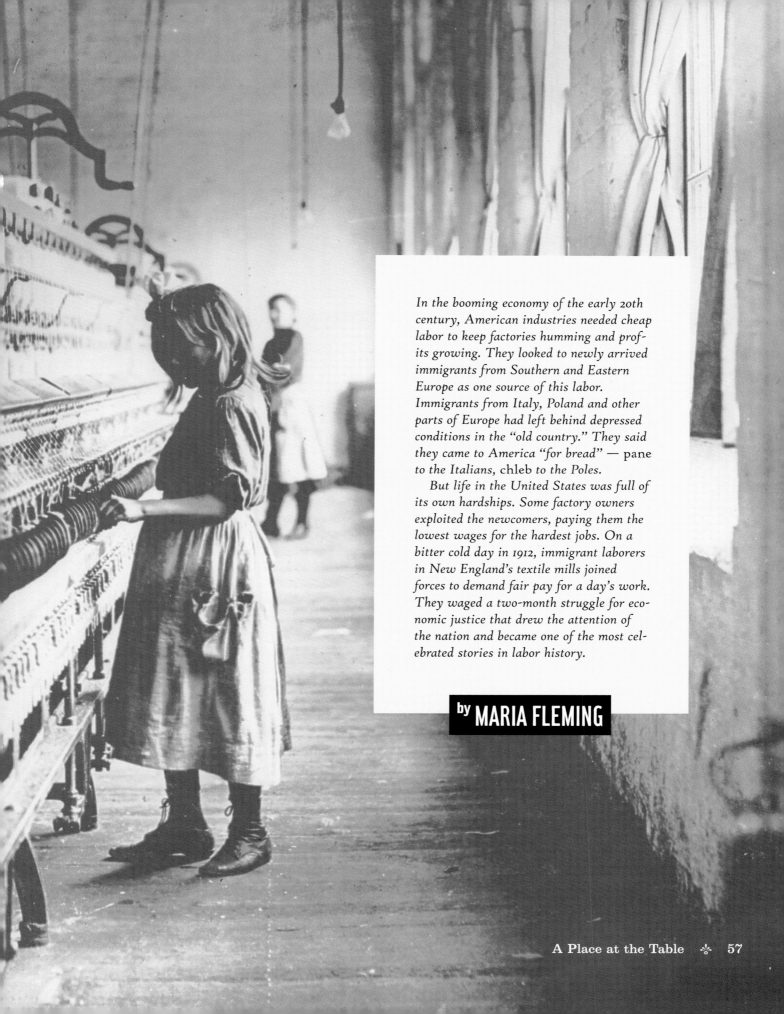

In the booming economy of the early 20th century, American industries needed cheap labor to keep factories humming and profits growing. They looked to newly arrived immigrants from Southern and Eastern Europe as one source of this labor. Immigrants from Italy, Poland and other parts of Europe had left behind depressed conditions in the "old country." They said they came to America "for bread" — pane to the Italians, chleb to the Poles.

But life in the United States was full of its own hardships. Some factory owners exploited the newcomers, paying them the lowest wages for the hardest jobs. On a bitter cold day in 1912, immigrant laborers in New England's textile mills joined forces to demand fair pay for a day's work. They waged a two-month struggle for economic justice that drew the attention of the nation and became one of the most celebrated stories in labor history.

by **MARIA FLEMING**

January 12, 1912, began like every other day for 14-year-old Carmella Teoli. The sleep-shattering screech of the factory whistle roused her from bed at dawn. The whistle regulated life in the textile city of Lawrence, Massachusetts, telling laborers when to wake up, when to begin work and when to return home. Carmella dressed hurriedly and ate a meager breakfast of bread and molasses. When the whistle blew again, Carmella and her father shuffled to the hulking textile mills where they worked.

Since the early 1800s, many textile cities had sprouted up in New England's green valleys. But Lawrence reigned as queen of the milltowns. Almost a dozen textile factories lined its riverbanks, with more than 40,000 people laboring in the mills. Most of the workers, including Carmella Teoli and her father, were recent immigrants from Europe. Wood Mill, where Carmella worked, was the largest worsted wool mill in the world. More than a third of a mile long, with 30 acres of floor space, Wood Mill alone employed 10,000 workers.

Carmella had left school in the 6th grade, when she was 12, to work in the mills. Her family needed the $6.55 she could earn each week to help support

Carmella and her four brothers and sisters. Laws prohibited children younger than 14 from working in factories. But poor families and mill owners often found ways around these laws.

The Teoli family had emigrated from Italy to America when Carmella was 3 years old. Italian immigrants were not the only ones who came to New England seeking jobs. Poles, Turks, Russians, Greeks, Syrians, Portuguese, Lithuanians and dozens of other nationalities flocked to Lawrence to work in the mills.

Immigrants like the Teolis were sometimes drawn to New England by advertisements placed by American mill owners in their native towns. One poster prominently displayed in an Italian village depicted a happy family, laden with bags of gold, marching into Lawrence's Wood Mill. "No one goes hungry in Lawrence. Here all can work, all can eat," the poster read.

The reality of life in Lawrence was a far cry from the pretty picture on the poster, however. The average 16 cents an hour that workers earned barely kept a family in bread, let alone gold. Meat,

Laws prohibited the employment of children younger than 14 in the factories, but poor families and mill owners found ways around the laws.

ing cotton and wool into yarn and yarn into cloth. The steady roar of the machines was deafening.

Carmella Teoli worked as a doffer. Doffers scrambled over the huge machinery, replacing bobbins full of newly spun thread with empty ones. Many other children worked in the mills, too. Some worked as burlers, cutting knots out of cloth. Others were sweepers, clearing away lint and wool that covered the floor like drifts of snow.

Mill jobs required sharp eyes and quick fingers. If Carmella found a break in the thread, she had to fix it fast by tying the ends together. But workers had to be careful. Sometimes fingers got caught in the machinery and snapped like the threads. Machines also mangled arms and legs — or worse.

One day, Carmella's long hair got tangled in some gears of a machine and a patch of her scalp was ripped from her head. Co-workers wrapped the skin in newspaper and rushed Carmella to the hospital. After her wound healed, Carmella wore her hair in a bun to hide the 6-inch scar the accident had left.

Millwork was also known for its hidden dangers. The humid, lint-choked air wasn't safe to breathe. Many people contracted pneumonia, tuberculosis and other respiratory diseases. The death rate for millworkers was so high that a third of young millworkers never made it to their 25th birthday.

For their efforts, the average laborers earned poverty wages — about $8.75 a week, barely enough to cover rent and food.

butter and milk were all luxuries. Workers couldn't afford the fine wool fabric they spent their days making; they dressed instead in thin, worn clothing.

Many of the immigrants lived crammed together in a slum called "the Plains." The mill operators owned many of the tenements the immigrants lived in and charged high rents. Some families took boarders in their already crowded apartments to help meet expenses. Usually, every room had at least one bed, including the kitchen.

Garbage-lined streets, rats and other unsanitary conditions in the Plains left its residents prone to diseases such as typhoid and cholera. "The mortality in the crowded tenement districts, especially in the summer . . . reads like battle statistics," reported the *Lawrence Evening Tribune.*

Each morning, workers left the dismal tenements for the dismal mills. The cavernous factory rooms were alive with noise and motion — clicking spindles, whirling bobbins, thundering looms — all turn-

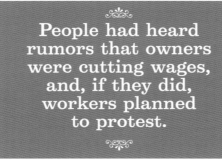

People had heard rumors that owners were cutting wages, and, if they did, workers planned to protest.

Perhaps the worst part of millwork was the grinding tedium — endless hours of the same dreary work, day after day. But for Carmella and other workers, this particular snowy Friday at the Wood Mill felt different. There was an undercurrent of tension and excitement in the air. People had heard rumors that owners were cutting wages, and, if they did, workers planned to protest.

A new law was at the root of the trouble. Beginning January 1, the state had ordered mill owners to reduce the work week from 56 to 54 hours. In the past, when hours had been cut, managers also slashed wages. They made up for lost time with "speed-ups" and "stretch-outs"; employees had to

tend a larger number of machines operating at a faster rate, making the labor even more exhausting. So laborers simply ended up doing the same or more work for less money.

But today, January 12, was the first payday at Wood Mill since the law had gone into effect. The previous day, at the Everett Mill, a group of Polish women stormed off the job when they found a shortage in their pay envelopes. Now there were murmurings that if the other mills cut wages, too, there would be a mass strike in all the factories.

When the paymaster blew his whistle, Carmella and the other employees gathered anxiously around to collect their wages. They tore their envelopes open. Suddenly the mill erupted with shouts of "Short pay! Strike! All out!" Someone pulled a switch halting the bobbins in their spinning frames. Workers ran through the factory cutting belts on the machines, smashing gears and hurling bobbins and

shuttles. Carmella Teoli joined the growing crowd of workers as they swarmed out of the mill, still shouting, "Strike! Short pay! Strike!"

The strike soon spread to the nearby Washington Mill, where Carmella's father worked. Soon, several thousand more laborers spilled onto the streets. Angry workers from the Washington and Wood mills then marched to the Ayer Mill where they broke through the gates and called on others to join the walkout. By noon on Friday, the strike swelled to 11,000 millworkers.

The deduction from the workers' pay envelopes amounted to about 32 cents, roughly the cost of three loaves of bread. But for these immigrants eking out a living, it was a significant sum. What some workers came to call "the struggle for the three loaves" had begun.

That night, Angelo Rocco, a high school student and weaver for the American Woolen Company,

sent a telegram to the New York headquarters of the Industrial Workers of the World (IWW), a radical labor union. Rocco, an Italian immigrant, asked for the IWW's help in sustaining the strike until laborers' demands were met.

The IWW, known as the Wobblies, was a controversial group. Its mission was to unite working people everywhere in an effort to eliminate what its members called a system of "slave wages." They thought that the laborers who produced the world's goods should control the factories and reap the profits of industry.

While other unions such as the American Federation of Labor often discriminated against unskilled laborers from Asia and southeastern Europe, the Wobblies sought to bring together all workers. The Wobblies meant different things to different people: To some, they were a group of dangerous anarchists trying to wage a class war; to others, they were champions of justice and the one true friend of laborers.

Wobbly activist Joe Ettor, a fiery speaker who had organized strikes in shipyards, lumber mills and coal mines across the country, responded to the call for help. He arrived in Lawrence that weekend and immediately started organizing protesters.

Ettor knew that factory owners often used ethnic tensions to divide workers, paying some immigrant groups lower wages than others and threatening to replace workers of one nationality with workers of another. Mill executives hoped that creating such rivalries would prevent workers from forming unions.

To build unity among the 45 different ethnic groups the strikers represented, Ettor cautioned workers to "forget that you are Hebrews, forget that you are Poles, Germans, or Russians." Ettor formed a strike committee that included representatives from the different cultural groups. The committee presented its demands to the mill owners: a 15 percent increase in pay, overtime pay and a promise that no strikers would suffer penalties when they returned to work.

As some of the strikers engaged Wobbly support, city officials in Lawrence called for military backup. Hundreds of state police and militia, armed with bayonets, streamed into Lawrence to help control the crowds. News of the strike made front page headlines around the country as people waited to see what would happen in Lawrence.

Mill owners predicted that most of the belligerent workers would settle down and return to their factory posts after the weekend. But they were wrong. On Monday, January 15, in the midst of a snowstorm, 8,000 picketing strikers swirled around the Washington and Wood mills in an effort to prevent others from returning to work. Protesters were ruthless toward scabs, workers who refused to join the strike. They spat at the scabs, doused them with scalding water, dumped pails of garbage on them, tore off their coats, grabbed their lunch pails — anything to keep people from breaking the picket lines.

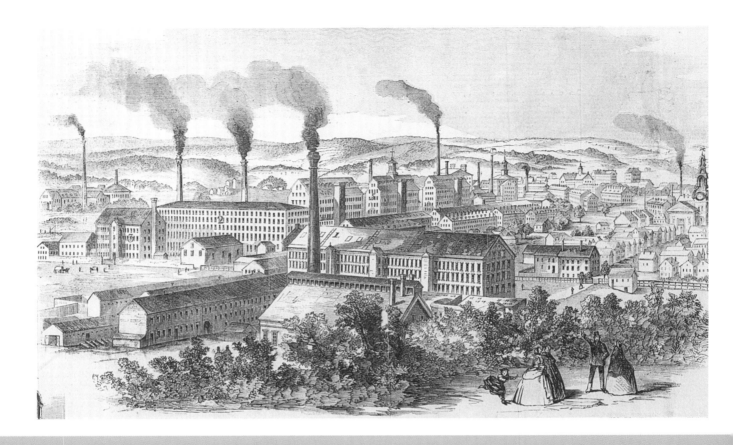

DOCUMENT

UNITED WE STAND

The coming together of diverse ethnic groups during the Lawrence strike was an unusual event, although not unprecedented. In 1903, two groups of immigrant field laborers joined forces to form a union, the Japanese-Mexican Labor Association (JMLA) in Oxnard, Calif. The JMLA was the first major agricultural labor union in the United States formed by different minority groups.

After launching a successful strike protesting wage cuts for workers in Oxnard's sugar beet fields, the JMLA sought membership in the American Federation of Labor (AFL). The AFL was the nation's largest union. J. M. Lizarras, the Mexican secretary of the JMLA, petitioned the AFL for a charter, which AFL President Samuel Gompers said he would grant with one stipulation: The Mexican union

members must drop the Japanese laborers from their ranks. It was a dictate that reflected the pervasive prejudice against Asians during this period in U.S. history.

The Mexican branch of the JMLA refused to consent to Gompers's demand. In a letter rejecting the charter, Lizarras eloquently described the kinship that bound the workers together.

We have counseled, fought and lived on very short rations with our Japanese brothers, and toiled with them in the fields, and they have been uniformly kind and considerate. We would be false to them and to ourselves and the cause of unionism if we now accepted privileges for ourselves which are not accorded to them. We are going to stand by men who stood by us in the long, hard fight which ended in a victory over the enemy. We therefore respectfully petition the A.F. of L. to grant us a charter under which we can unite all the sugar beet and field laborers in Oxnard without regard to their color or race. We will refuse any other kind of charter, except one which will wipe out race prejudices and recognize our fellow workers as being as good as ourselves. . . .

(Left) Lawrence reigned as queen of the milltowns, with more than a dozen textile factories lining its riverbanks. (Below) Garbage-lined streets, rats and other unsanitary conditions in the slum known as the Plains left its residents prone to infectious diseases.

The crowd surged to 15,000 women, men and children. Protesters marched to the Prospect Mill, then on to the Atlantic and the Pacific mills, with plans to storm the gates and shut the mills down. Police and militia turned them back with bayonets and fire hoses. Strikers threw stones, coal and chunks of ice at law enforcers and mill windows. The rioting continued throughout the week. "Real Labor War Now in Lawrence," *The New York Times* declared.

City leaders denounced this rebellion by "ignorant foreigners." In a meeting with one of the strike leaders, Lawrence Mayor Michael A. Scanlon fumed, "I want you to understand that a crowd of bandits is not going to run this city. I will keep order here if I have to call on the whole Federal Army, and believe me when I tell you that if today's riots are repeated tomorrow, there will be an awful slaughter."

But the city's efforts to thwart the protesters merely spurred them on. "They will need five million militiamen to keep track of our pickets," organizer Joe Ettor challenged. He accused officials of tricking people into returning to work by announcing that the strike had ended. Even if they succeeded in thinning strikers' ranks, Ettor said, the mill owners would still pay a price. "We will cripple

We Built This Country

Beginning in the 1880s, the pattern of immigration into the Eastern U.S. shifted. Many Americans voiced alarm that the new wave of immigrants arriving from Italy, Poland, Russia and other countries of Southern and Eastern Europe would "mongrelize Nordic-American Stock." In 1924, Congress passed the National Origins Act, a quota system that greatly favored immigration from northwestern Europe. Both before and after the bill became law, immigrants from the targeted countries denounced it. Following is an excerpt from a letter sent by the Slovak League of America to the Senate Committee on Immigration protesting the quota system, which would remain in place until 1965.

The Slovaks entered the most hazardous vocations — coal mining and steel making — and they contributed their share toward the gigantic growth and development of these industries, which are so important to the life of this country. But they did more than merely work and enhance industrial and commercial values. They built churches and national halls; . . . they organized fraternal beneficial societies. . . . They have bought farms and cultivated them with such results that the secretaries of agriculture . . . sing unstinted praise of the Slovak farmers, who, to use the phraseology of one such report, have practically coaxed crops out of rocks. . . . They built thereon their houses, and always have gardens and flowers. . . .

They have given unmistakable proof of their love for this country in the days of the world war. . . .

In view of the above, we ask: Is it consistent with the policies and principles of the United States to discriminate against such a fine type of people who seek this country because in it they can realize their dreams . . . ? Is it in accord with those blazing ideas of democracy which were so forcefully expressed by the founders of this great republic and which have become an heirloom not only of America but of the whole civilized world?

their machinery," he threatened. "God pity their looms. God pity their cloth."

By the middle of January, 25,000 workers from 11 mills were on strike — more than half of them women and children. Strikers formed human chains around the mills. They organized huge parades. Marchers carried banners reading "We Strike for Justice." Immigrants dressed their children in red, white and blue and waved U.S. flags, along with the flags of their homelands, to link their struggle with the ideals of their adopted country. The protesters shouted, sang anthems, clanged tin pans, blared horns and rang cow bells as they wound their way through the streets, calling to bystanders to join them.

A Wobbly writer described the power of the demonstrations: "It is the first strike I ever saw which sang. They are always marching and singing. The tired, gray crowds ebbing and flowing perpetually into the mills had waked and opened their mouths to sing. I shall not soon forget the curious lift, the strange sudden fire of the mingled nationalities at the strike meetings when they broke into the universal language of song."

The strike dragged on through the winter. On February 10, a violent conflict erupted between authorities and some of the protesters. Police

Newspaper accounts of police brutality at the Lawrence strike prompted a public outcry.

"Bread and Roses"

About a decade after the strike at Lawrence, Wobbly writer James Oppenheim commemorated the event with this poem. He said it was inspired by a woman striker who carried a sign during one of the protests that read, "We want bread and roses too." He thought this sentiment captured the essence of the mill workers' struggle to escape some of the hardships of factory life. The poem, like the strike, became world-famous. It has since been put to music and workers have embraced it as their own rallying cry during later labor protests. Today, because of the poem, the 1912 walkout in the Lawrence mills is remembered as "the strike for bread and roses."

As we come marching, marching in the beauty of the day,
A million darkened kitchens, a thousand mill lofts gray,
And touched with all the radiance that a sudden sun discloses,
For the people hear us singing: "Bread and roses! Bread and roses!"

As we come marching, marching, we battle too for men,
For they are women's children, and we mother them again.
Our lives shall not be sweated from birth until life closes;
Hearts starve as well as bodies; give us bread, but give us roses!

As we come marching, marching, unnumbered women dead
Go crying through our singing their ancient cry for bread.
Small art and love and beauty their drudging spirits knew.
Yes, it is bread we fight for — but we fight for roses, too!

As we come marching, marching, we bring the greater days.
The rising of the women means the rising of the race.
No more the drudge and idler — ten that toil where one reposes,
But a sharing of life's glories: Bread and roses! Bread and roses!

During a New York mill strike in 1916, a Polish immigrant evicted from her residence set up her cookstove outdoors.

were accused of assaulting women and children. Newspaper accounts of the bloody encounter prompted a public outcry, and Congress called for an investigation.

Some of the millworkers — 16 children and a handful of adults — traveled to Washington, D.C., to testify before a legislative committee about the incident. "I saw policemen clubbing women on their hearts and breasts; women being in the family way were arrested and dragged and pushed into the patrol wagon," one strike organizer reported. "I saw them take little children and pick them up by the leg and throw them in the patrol wagon like they were rags."

Children described the terrible working conditions in the mill. They also testified about how they lost an hour's wages if they were five minutes late for work, how they paid 10 cents every two weeks for drinking water, and how they cleaned the factories on Saturday mornings without pay.

Fourteen-year-old Carmella Teoli delivered the most dramatic testimony of the proceedings. In stark words, she described to a stunned group of legislators and onlookers how the mill machinery had scalped her. She told of the seven months she spent in the hospital while her butchered head healed. She talked of the fluctuating wages her father brought home and of her family's dependence on her earnings. When asked why she had joined the strike in Lawrence, Carmella said simply, "Because I didn't get enough to eat at home."

The testimonies prompted President William Howard Taft to launch a national investigation into factory working conditions. Newspapers around the U.S. reported the children's testimony. A few days later, on March 12, the Lawrence mill owners — humiliated by the negative publicity and worn down by the financial strain of their factories' gutted workforce — gave in to the strikers' demands.

A victory parade through the streets of Lawrence marked the end of the laborers' nine-week struggle. The strikers' success rippled out to other communities as well, with factory owners throughout New England announcing pay raises for workers. Labor experts estimate that more than 250,000 workers benefited from the Lawrence protest.

The Myth of the Melting Pot

What is an American? How do we define our national identity? One idea that has persisted over generations is the image of America as a "melting pot" — a vast cauldron into which individuals from different backgrounds are tossed and, through some alchemy, emerge as one distinct people. But the truth is, that metaphor has never really fit. Certain groups in the United States were considered "unmeltable"; the mainstream culture — White, Christian, Western European — maintained that the races, religions, languages, traditions and values of these groups made them unable to become truly "Americans."

Because of their skin color alone, blacks were excluded by the dominant white culture from the melting pot metaphor. Some thought Indians might "learn to walk the white man's road" and could therefore be successfully incorporated into the mix; but others believed that Native peoples' "heathen" and "savage" ways made them undesirable.

The dominant culture also worried that certain immigrant groups would dilute the white racial stock. Darker-skinned immigrants from Mexico and southeastern Europe were greeted with suspicion. Asian immigrants, like men and women of African descent, were rejected outright from the nation's melting pot. And even those immigrants who were deemed acceptable were expected to abandon their native cultures so that they might better blend into American society.

But even if their skin color and "alien" customs and beliefs prevented them from "melting" into the mainstream culture, groups that had been pushed to the margins of American society still demanded to participate in its civic culture. They fought to be recognized as citizens, to vote, to testify in court and serve on juries. And as they won these rights, assimilation became beside the point. In the eyes of the law, they were Americans.

Recognizing the limitations of the metaphor of the melting pot, American writers, historians and political leaders in recent years have offered alternate visions of our national identity: America as a mosaic, a kaleidoscope, a tapestry — even a salad bowl. In each of these images, the different parts retain their unique characteristics but, in coming together, create something new.

Jesse Jackson, U.S. political leader and a lifelong civil rights activist, described his view of our nation: "America is not like a blanket — one piece of unbroken cloth, the same color, the same texture, the same size. America is more like a quilt — many pieces, many colors, many sizes, all woven and held together by a common thread."

These new metaphors allow us to acknowledge and value our differences — in physical appearance, history, custom, language, religion — and yet affirm that there is still something that unites us as a nation. Once that "glue" was widely believed to be a core culture, Western European in origin. Now it is generally recognized as a commitment to a set of ideals: democracy, freedom of religion and expression, equality.

Our differences themselves can even be a source of national pride and unity. The abundance of cultures that constitute our nation is unique in all the world. As Walt Whitman wrote in a poetic tribute to America's pluralism, "Of every hue and caste am I, of every rank and religion/I resist anything better than my own diversity."

Angelo Rocco, who played an active role in the 1912 strike, would later recall how he and other rebelling workers were described by newspaper reporters and city officials during the demonstrations. "[They] always called me un-American, an immigrant or an alien," Rocco said. "Of course, I felt myself to be much more American than they were. They thought it was American to believe in exploitation. I thought it was American to believe in the Constitution."

In the end, the workers who rose up to march and sing and struggle in the name of justice during the bitter winter of 1912 averaged less than a dollar increase in their weekly wages. But the battle in the mills of Lawrence was about more than money; it was also about human dignity and the value of work. The Lawrence millworkers were poor immigrants who, having clothed their adopted nation through endless hours of grueling labor, voiced their ardent wish to become part of the fabric of America. They sought for themselves and their families their rightful place at the table, as well as the right to put on that table *pane* — *chleb* — bread. ☒

6

Cross-Country ⚜ 1915

ROAD TRIP FOR SUFFRAGE

VOTES FOR US WHEN WE ARE WOMEN

VOTES FOR US
- WHEN -
WE ARE WOMEN

In 1848, a small group of women issued a Declaration of Sentiments in Seneca Falls, New York, and ushered in the organized women's rights movement in the United States. It would take decades of unwavering effort by legions of women to attain one of the Declaration's demands: the right to vote. As the suffrage battle wore on, women's rights activists grew increasingly impatient. In the early 1900s, a new generation of suffragists energized the movement with dramatic demonstrations, including parades, pageants and other public spectacles. In 1915, these more militant suffragists organized a daring cross-country auto trip to promote women's voting rights. The trio of suffrage pilgrims chosen to make the journey would soon discover that the road to justice can be a bumpy one.

by HARRIET SIGERMAN

On a stormy night in October 1915, three women drove through the desolate Kansas plains in a downpour, hoping to get to Emporia before morning. It was late, and they had the road to themselves. Suddenly, their car lurched and stopped: They had driven right into a mud hole and were stuck. The car would not budge — it just sank deeper and deeper in the mud.

The travelers cried out for help, but their pleas evaporated in the howling wind and rain. Finally, one of the women remembered seeing a farmhouse two or three miles back. She climbed out of the car and, bending forward to brace herself against the wind, started walking. With every step, she sank knee-deep in the soggy ground, and her brown wool suit and high heels were soon covered with mud.

"How had the journey come to this?" Sara Bard Field must have wondered as she struggled through the wind and rain. Only a few weeks before, on September 16, Field had stood in a grand hall decked out in colorful banners and ribbons and crowded with more than 1,000 women. The occasion was a majestic ceremony marking the end of a three-day

women's rights convention in San Francisco, California, and the beginning of a historic cross-country trip that Field was undertaking to publicize the cause of women's suffrage.

As the ceremony drew to a close, Field had climbed into a waiting car covered with streamers. Then, to the cheers and whistles of the crowd, she and her traveling companions had driven off into the foggy night. Their mission: to carry an enormous petition across the country pledging support for a federal women's suffrage amendment to the Constitution. The women would make stops along the way to rally support for the amendment and add signatures to the petition before delivering it to President Woodrow Wilson and the U.S. Congress.

The journey would also serve a symbolic purpose. In 1915, twelve Western states — with their more enlightened social and legal institutions and a long tradition of women's social activism — had already granted women the right to vote. Field, who hailed from one of these states, Oregon, represented a movement of four million Western women voters demanding the same political rights for their disenfranchised Eastern sisters, via a federal amendment.

Now, as she sloshed toward a remote farmhouse in the wilderness, Field did not feel like someone who symbolized the political hopes and dreams of so many American women. After trudging through the wind and rain for two hours, she finally stumbled upon the farmhouse she had seen from the road.

Soaking wet and caked with mud, she explained her predicament to the sleepy-eyed farmer who opened the door. He hitched up two sturdy workhorses to his truck and drove Field back to the stalled car. On the way, she explained the purpose of her cross-country trip. The farmer seemed somewhat baffled by Field's description of their mission and simply responded, "Well, you girls have guts."

Indeed, it had taken pluck and courage to make such a journey and endure the harsh road conditions. In 1915, cars were still a luxury item that few people could afford. Cross-country excursions were considered risky. There were no superhighways and few gas stations, restaurants and other conveniences along the way. Most roads were little more than dusty, poorly marked two-lane byways. In fact, never before had a group of women driven alone across the United States. The announcement of the journey had created a sensation, capturing

The organizers of the road trip publicized Field's efforts nationwide.

newspaper headlines around the country — just as its organizers had intended.

Field had been hand-picked to make the journey by the leaders of the Congressional Union, the militant branch of the National American Woman Suffrage Association (NAWSA). She was an ideal choice for the task. Petite and youthful, Field was poised and personable in front of large crowds. Born in Cincinnati, Ohio, in 1882, she first became active in women's suffrage after she moved to Oregon with her husband, a minister. She became a paid state organizer for NAWSA and soon emerged as an eloquent and charismatic speaker for the Western suffrage movement.

The work was grueling. Field spoke on street corners throughout countless small towns, snatched whatever rest she could and ate on the run. Meanwhile, she divorced her husband, who opposed her suffrage work and expected her to devote herself to the duties of a minister's wife. She reclaimed her maiden name and joined the Congressional Union to work for a Constitutional amendment for women's

(Top) Before entering each town, the women decorated the car with a suffrage banner. *(Above)* In the early 1900s, a new generation of suffragists energized the movement with dramatic public spectacles.

suffrage — the same demand firmly expressed in the petition she now carried across the country.

Accompanying Field on the transcontinental trip were Ingeborg Kindstedt and Maria Kindberg, two Swedish immigrant women who were also ardent suffragists. They owned the car and would serve as driver and mechanic. Mabel Vernon, also of the Congressional Union, traveled ahead of the convoy by train; like a silent scout paving the way, she organized parades, rallies and receptions for Field's arrival.

Suffragist leaders considered Sara Bard Field an ideal choice for the cross-country campaign.

The first leg of the journey took the women through California, Nevada and Utah, then on through Wyoming, Colorado and Kansas. Enthusiastic crowds greeted the travelers at dozens of stops along the way. Before entering each town, the women decorated the car with purple, gold and white flags and with a suffrage banner that read: "We Demand an Amendment to the Constitution of the United States, Enfranchising Women."

In some cities, suffrage workers welcomed the voyagers with huge motorcades, bands, fireworks and other pageantry. Women thronged around the car to add their names to the growing petition. Governors, mayors and congressmen greeted the suffrage envoys at formal receptions, and Field succeeded in persuading some to sign the petition as well.

The Rights of Women

Among the 300 delegates to the Seneca Falls women's rights convention were 31 men, one of whom was abolitionist Frederick Douglass. While Douglass's primary objective during his life was attaining freedom and equality for African Americans, he spoke up repeatedly on behalf of women's rights. Following is an excerpt from an editorial that appeared in the July 28, 1848, edition of his antislavery newspaper The North Star *in response to criticism of the Seneca Falls convention.*

We are not insensible that the bare mention of this truly important subject in any other than terms of contemptuous ridicule and scornful disfavor, is likely to excite against us the fury of bigotry and the folly of prejudice. A discussion of the rights of animals would be regarded with far more complacency by many of what are called the "wise" and the "good" of our land, than would a discussion of the rights of women. . . .

Many who have at last made the discovery that the negroes have some rights as well as other members of the human family, have yet to be convinced that women are entitled to any. Eight years ago a number of persons of this description actually abandoned the anti-slavery cause, lest by giving their influence in that direction they might possibly be giving countenance to the dangerous heresy that woman, in respect to rights, stands on an equal footing with man.

In the judgement of such persons the American slave system, with all its concomitant horrors, is less to be deplored than this "wicked" idea. It is perhaps needless to say, that we cherish little sympathy for such sentiments or respect for such prejudices. Standing as we do up on the watch-tower of human freedom, we cannot be deterred from an expression of our approbation of any movement, however humble, to improve and elevate the character of any members of the human family. . . .

[W]e hold woman to be justly entitled to all we claim for man. We go farther, and express our conviction that all political rights which it is expedient for man to exercise, it is equally so for woman. All that distinguishes man as an intelligent and accountable being, is equally true of woman, and if that government only is just which governs by the free consent of the governed, there can be no reason in the world for denying to woman the exercise of the elective franchise, or a hand in making and administering the laws of the land.

Our doctrine is that "right is of no sex." We therefore bid the women engaged in this movement our humble Godspeed.

At every stop, Field gave impassioned speeches. In Colorado Springs, she aimed a stinging rebuke at opponents of women's suffrage, especially men.

"[T]hey are very slow in awaking to the fact that the womanhood is being wasted in the struggle for enfranchisement, when it could be used to better advantage in creating a real civilization," Field chided. "Steam cars and airships do not make a civilization, but give woman the ballot and she will use it as a tool for the upbuilding of civilization, such as the world has never seen before."

As the travellers passed through small towns and villages, curious onlookers often gathered to see the banner-bedecked car rumble by. Never missing an opportunity to win a convert to the suffrage cause, Field sometimes stopped at street corners to deliver an impromptu speech from the back of the car.

The trip was exhilarating — and exhausting. The women drove through rain, sleet and dust storms. They endured frigid temperatures, flat tires, engine difficulties and temper flare-ups. Outside Reno, Nev., the voyagers spent an entire day lost, without a map, in the stretch of barren land known as the "Great American Desert." On several occasions, the women had to get out and push the car through huge snowdrifts to make it to the next stop on time. But buoyed by the outpouring of support, and the importance of their cause, they pressed on.

Not every reception was a warm one, however. Women's suffrage was, after all, an issue that divided households, as well as the nation. As the women progressed eastward, they prepared themselves for their entry into "enemy territory" — those states that had rejected legislation giving women the vote.

As Field told a gathering in Kansas City, "Hard times still are ahead of us. Up till now we have been traveling in suffrage states, and it is hard to readjust ourselves now to the attitude of men who say, 'No, we don't want women to vote because they don't get up and give us their seats in streetcars.' I'd rather have a seat of justice than a streetcar seat, anyway."

After stops in Nebraska, Iowa and Missouri, Field got a taste of those hard times in Chicago, Illinois. There, a massive crowd of supporters turned out to meet Field and her companions. Scattered throughout the audience, however, were some suffrage opponents — "antis" — who tried to shout Field down as she delivered her speech.

A Mother's Advice

After receiving the approval of the U.S. Congress in 1919, the women's suffrage amendment was sent to the states for ratification. In August of 1920, Tennessee became the 36th state to endorse the controversial amendment, and it passed into law. Harry Burn, a young state congressman from Tennessee, had cast the deciding vote. At first, Burn had been uncertain how to vote, but ultimately he gave in to a request from his mother — a devoted suffragist — to back the measure. Below are excerpts from a letter that Mrs. J. L. Burn sent to her son before the vote and from her son's statement defending his decision to the Tennessee House of Representatives.

Hurrah! And vote for suffrage and don't keep them in doubt. I notice some of the speeches against. They were very bitter. I have been watching to see how you stood, but have noticed nothing yet. Don't forget to be a good boy and help Mrs. Catt* put 'Rat' in Ratification.
— Mrs. J. L. Burn
to her son

GIVE MOTHER THE VOTE
WE NEED IT

VOTES FOR OUR MOTHERS

OUR FOOD   OUR HEALTH   OUR PLAY
OUR HOMES OUR SCHOOLS OUR WORK
ARE RULED BY MEN'S VOTES

Isn't it a funny thing
That Father cannot see
Why Mother ought to have a vote
On how these things should be?

THINK IT OVER

I want to state that I changed my vote in favor of ratification first because I believe in full suffrage as a right; second, I believe we had a moral and legal right to ratify; third, I knew that a mother's advice is always safest for her boy to follow and my mother wanted me to vote for ratification; fourth, I appreciated the fact that an opportunity such as seldom comes to a mortal man to free seventeen million women from political slavery was mine.
— Congressman Harry Burn to the Tennessee
House of Representatives

*Carrie Chapman Catt, president of the National American Woman Suffrage Association

"The women were the worst opposers," Field said later, "the right-wing DAR [Daughters of the American Revolution] and all associations of that kind were extremely anti, and they sent their speakers right on my trail in the East."

Despite these new difficulties, the hardy band of travelers continued on, making stops in Indiana, Ohio and Michigan before heading to Albany, the capital of New York. Reports of Field's exploits had reached the state's governor, who greeted the suffrage crusader in the executive mansion. He paid the diminutive Field the highest compliment of all: "I thought you would be ten feet tall." He then signed the petition, despite the recent defeat of women's suffrage by the male voters of New York State.

But Sara Bard Field felt neither tall nor powerful. Instead, she was tense and exhausted after traveling two months in a crowded car over bumpy, pitted roads, making countless speeches, stopping in a different town or city almost every day. And she still had most of the East Coast to cover.

To make matters worse, Field had a frightening confrontation with one of her traveling companions, Ingeborg Kindstedt. One day while they were driving along, Kindstedt complained that Field was making all the speeches and grabbing all the attention. Field pointed out that English was not Kindstedt's native tongue, which would be a disadvantage in addressing crowds.

But Kindstedt could not be placated. She shot Field a withering glance and spat the words out like bullets: "I am going to kill you before we get to the end of this journey." Field was scared, but she couldn't believe that Kindstedt was serious. Still, she kept a wary eye on her companion for the rest of the journey.

Starving for the Right to Vote

IN CONTEXT

After completing her historic cross-country trip, Sara Bard Field helped organize the National Woman's Party (NWP) in 1916. The NWP absorbed the Congressional Union and embraced its militant philosophy. Unlike its larger sister organization, the National American Woman Suffrage Association (NAWSA), the NWP was not content just to circulate petitions, write letters to newspapers and elected officials, and engage in other lawful means of campaigning for suffrage. Nor did it agree with NAWSA's approach of trying to secure women's suffrage state-by-state. Instead, the NWP fought for a federal suffrage amendment to enfranchise all American women at once and used confrontation and pressure to achieve its ends.

Fed up with President Woodrow Wilson's foot-dragging over supporting a federal women's suffrage amendment, the NWP started sending pickets to the White House in 1916. For the next year and a half, in snowstorms and torrential rain, and during Washington's hot, humid summers, the NWP pickets protested in front of the White House. The demonstrators ranged in age from young college women to grandmothers in their 80s, and they carried eye-catching banners demanding justice. "Mr. President, how long must women wait for liberty?" read one sign. But the White House gates were clamped shut, and Wilson ignored them.

Women came from across the nation to help picket, and if they couldn't come, they sent a representative. Mrs. S. H. B. Gray of Colorado wrote, "I have no son to give my country to fight for democracy abroad, and so I send my daughter to Washington to fight for democracy at home."

At first, the public eagerly supported the pickets. But after the United States entered World War I in April 1917, public support turned to hostility. Any form of dissent against the government was considered treasonous. The police began to arrest the demonstrators, usually on the flimsy charge of obstructing traffic.

After a quick succession of stops in Massachusetts, Rhode Island, New York City, Delaware and Maryland, the weary travelers approached their last stop: Washington, D.C. They had spent nearly three months on the road, logging more than 5,000 miles and collecting a half-million signatures for their petition.

The women prepared the valiant little car — now dented and scratched and covered with stickers from every stop — for its entrance into the nation's capital. Shortly after 11:00 a.m. on December 6, 1915, the car moved slowly down the Baltimore Turnpike, like a war-weary soldier triumphantly marching into the final battle. Across its dusty front fender stretched a vivid purple streamer with the words emblazoned in white, "On to Congress." The car stopped just outside the city.

There, they were met by a welcoming committee befitting royalty. Undaunted by the bitterly cold weather, the crowd assembled for a parade through downtown Washington. As a band began to play, Mrs. John Jay White, the grand marshal, led the way on horseback, holding her riding crop aloft like a torch. Behind her came Field and her fellow envoys in the battered car that had carried them across a continent and now toward their final destinations, the Capitol and the White House.

> **Scores of other women proudly followed, waving their pennants at the cheering crowds along the way.**

Judges sentenced some women while dismissing others. But suffragists refused to recognize the court's authority over them. NWP leader Alice Paul sternly informed one judge: "We do not consider ourselves subject to this court, since as an unenfranchised class we have nothing to do with the making of the laws which have put us in this position." Judges beseeched the demonstrators to pay the fines — only a few dollars — but they almost always chose imprisonment instead. About 168 women served time in prison, many in Occoquan Workhouse in Virginia.

Jail conditions were dreadful. The picketers endured spoiled, wormy food; filthy sheets and blankets; putrid open toilets that could be flushed only from outside their cells and thus at the whim of guards; rats and cockroaches; lack of ventilation; and even solitary confinement.

Some picketers went on a hunger strike to protest the violation of their right to see a lawyer and their treatment as criminals instead of political prisoners. In response, jail authorities resorted to forced feeding.

Lucy Burns, the chief organizer in the NWP, was fed through the nose. She managed to smuggle a note out of jail describing her ordeal: "Was stretched on bed . . . [and] held down by five people at legs, arms and head. I refused to open mouth. Gannon pushed the tube up left nostril. I turned and twisted my head all I could, but he managed to push it up. It hurt nose and throat very much and makes nose bleed freely. Tube drawn out covered with blood."

From August to November 1917, the abusive treatment by prison authorities worsened. One night in November — later known as "the Night of Terror" — the guards at Occoquan Workhouse savagely beat the suffragists. Among the prisoners was Dorothy Day, radical journalist and social reformer. Two guards wrenched Day's arms above her head, lifted her up and slammed her body twice over the back of an iron bench. Lucy Burns was handcuffed to her cell door and threatened with a gag when she protested. Guards threw other suffragists against the wall of a cell; one even suffered a heart attack but was denied medical care.

The NWP skillfully publicized the picketers' plight. They asked congressmen to visit the prisons and sent out speakers, who shared with audiences accounts of fresh abuses. In December 1917, Wilson pardoned all of the suffragists, and the arrests ended temporarily. But by the summer of 1918, protesters were again arrested and jailed, and some went on hunger strikes, although prison officials refrained from using excessive force. The heroic suffragists who chose to go to prison risked losing not only their freedom but their lives for the right to vote.

Several women on foot carried the enormous petition, unrolled to only 100 of its almost 19,000 feet (more than three miles!). They were followed by more women on horseback, each rider representing one of the 12 states and Alaska Territory that had already granted women the right to vote. And behind them marched another group, representing the 36 states that had not yet granted that right. Next came flag and banner bearers dressed in purple and gold capes, their colors snapping smartly in the wind. They escorted a replica of the Liberty Bell decorated in purple, gold and white. Scores of other women proudly followed, waving their pennants at the cheering crowds along the way.

Finally, the parade reached the Capitol, where a large delegation of congressmen stood at the top of the polished white marble steps to receive Field. Slowly, she made her way to the delegation, followed by 20 women carrying the partially unrolled petition. Field, along with two pro-suffrage congressmen, spoke briefly, and the parade moved on to the White House. The procession of cars stopped in the semicircular drive in front of the president's mansion, and Field, her traveling companions and 300 other invited guests were ushered into the enormous East Room to be greeted by President Woodrow Wilson.

To Field, the president looked "stern and annoyed" — he had, after all, already endured similar pleas for a federal suffrage amendment from delegations of Eastern women and had told each of them in turn that women's suffrage was a matter for each state to decide, not a Constitutional question.

Beneath the huge, sparkling chandeliers, Field spoke first. "Mr. President, . . . I know what your stand [on suffrage] has been in the past. . . . But we have seen that, like all great men, you have changed your mind on other questions . . . and we honestly

(Left) Opponents of the suffrage movement organized to fight the amendment. *(Below)* Western states were the first to grant women the right to vote.

believe that circumstances have so altered that you may change your mind in this regard."

The women drew his attention to the petition, which Field had unrolled across the polished hardwood floor. Then Field gently but pointedly reminded him that many of the signatures came from governors, mayors and congressmen.

Wilson turned to Field, and said, "I hope it is true that I am not a man set stiffly beyond the possibility of learning. . . . Nothing could be more impressive than the presentation of such a request in such numbers and backed by such influences as undoubtedly stand behind you. . . .

"This visit of yours will remain in my mind not only as a delightful compliment, but also as a very impressive thing, which undoubtedly will make it

LOCKWOOD FOR PRESIDENT

In 1879, after a pitched battle, lawyer Belva Ann Lockwood became the first woman permitted to argue before the U.S. Supreme Court. Active in the suffrage movement, Lockwood refused to be thwarted by hurdles placed in front of her because of her gender.

"If women in the States are not permitted to vote, there is no law against their being voted for," Lockwood reasoned. And in 1884, she accepted the U.S. presidential nomination of the renegade Equal Rights Party. Lockwood knew she had no hope of winning the election, but she saw the symbolic significance of her candidacy and launched a vigorous campaign. In the end, she won more than 4,000 male votes and earned the electoral vote in Indiana. Following is an excerpt from her party platform.

In the furtherance of this purpose I have to say that *should* it be my good fortune to be elected, . . . it will be my earnest effort to promote and maintain equal political privileges to every class of our citizens irrespective of sex, color or nationality, and to make of this great and glorious Country in truth what it has so long

been in name, "the land of the free and the home of the brave."

I shall seek to insure a fair distribution of the public offices to women as well as to men, with a scrupulous regard to civil service reform after the women are duly installed in office. . . .

I am opposed to monopoly in the sense of the men of the country monopolizing all of the votes and all of the offices, and at the same time insisting upon having the distribution of all of the money both public and private. . . .

I am opposed to the wholesale monopoly of the judiciary of the country by the male voters. If elected, I shall feel it incumbent on me to appoint a reasonable number of women as District Attorneys, Marshals and Judges of United States Courts, and would appoint some competent woman to any vacancy that might occur on the United States Supreme Bench.

DOCUMENT

necessary for all of us to consider very carefully what is right for us to do."

But Field knew that he had not been persuaded. Later she said, "I could see at once that he would be a hard man to convince of anything that he did not spontaneously believe. But he *listened* to what you were saying. And his face — you could tell by his eyes that he was following what you said.

"Oh, the women went out jubilant. They thought this was the turning point. They thought he was going to back the amendment in Congress."

But, sadly, they were very wrong. As rumblings of war in Europe consumed the president's and the nation's attention, the federal suffrage amendment moved at

a snail's pace first through the House of Representatives and then through the U.S. Senate. Sara Bard Field and other dedicated suffragists did not give up the cause, however. In 1917, women won the right to vote in eight more states: North Dakota, Ohio, Indiana, Nebraska, Arkansas, Michigan, Rhode Island and New York. Field had visited most of these states during her cross-country tour. Whether her rallying efforts made the difference in those states remains unknown, but she surely helped to raise public awareness wherever she stopped.

World War I ended on November 11, 1918, and Congress soon took up the unfinished business of the women's suffrage amendment. On August 26, 1920, women's suffrage finally became the law of the land. It had been 72 years since American women

Struggle Within a Struggle

Although the leading suffrage organizations worked for equal rights under the law, they did not have the rights of all American women in mind. The National American Woman Suffrage Association (NAWSA) spurned African-American women's attempts to join the movement. A mixture of racism, resentment and political calculation led to this shameful chapter in American women's struggle for the right to vote.

The white suffragists' rejection of black women was a particularly bitter irony in light of the fact that the women's rights movement had grown out of the abolition movement. In the mid-1800s, many white women had been fierce opponents of slavery. However, they split from the abolition movement to create women's rights organizations when they found themselves shut out from leadership roles. After slavery was abolished and African-American men gained the vote in 1870 by way of the 15th amendment, white suffragists perceived black men to be making political gains at their expense, and their bitterness intensified.

Around 1900, growing numbers of white Southern women joined the suffrage movement. To appease them and win support for women's suffrage throughout the South, Northern suffragists began espousing racist ideas. They pointedly reminded white southerners that giving women the vote would prevent blacks from gaining too much political power, since there were more white women had met in Seneca Falls, New York, to demand their right to vote, and nearly five years since Sara Bard Field had made her momentous cross-country road trip.

As for Field, she remained active in the women's rights movement for a few more years. In 1920, she moved to San Francisco with her companion, the lawyer-poet Charles Erskine Scott Wood, and in 1938 they were married. Gradually, Field turned her energy from politics to poetry, and over the following two decades she published three volumes of verse. After her husband passed away, Field lived quietly in Berkeley, California, where she died on June 15, 1974.

Although she championed women's issues throughout her life, Field made her greatest contribution to women's social and political progress during her historic journey for justice. Like the larger movement that she represented, she surmounted obstacles and hardships along the way, and pushed on, undefeated, toward her goal. Years later she proudly declared, "The cross-country trip meant waking up a nation to national suffrage.... [W]e have made history." ☒

in the Southern states than black men and women combined. Even Sara Bard Field used this racist argument.

Unwelcome in the mainstream suffrage movement, African-American women formed their own suffrage organizations. They viewed the ballot as a powerful tool for improving their lives and communities. They also wanted to reclaim the political power lost by black men in Southern states that were violating their constitutional right to vote. By the early 1900s, black women's suffrage clubs had sprung up across the country, from New York and Massachusetts to Texas. Club members organized voter-education campaigns in their communities, circulated petitions calling for women's suffrage, worked in political campaigns and voted in states where they had the ballot.

Ida B. Wells-Barnett, a journalist and anti-lynching crusader, was a guiding spirit in the African-American women's suffrage movement. Petite in stature but a powerhouse of courage and determination, she lectured up and down the East Coast, establishing anti-lynching organizations and black women's clubs. In 1913, she organized the Alpha Suffrage Club of Chicago, the first African-American women's suffrage group in Illinois. She firmly believed that black women could use the ballot to end lynchings and other injustices against African Americans.

"With no sacredness of the ballot there can be no sacredness of human life itself," Wells wrote in one article. "For if the strong can take the weak man's ballot, when it suits his purpose to do so, he will take his life also."

In 1913, the Alpha Suffrage Club chose Wells-Barnett to march in a suffrage parade in Washington, D.C., sponsored by NAWSA. Eager to placate white delegates from the South, white suffrage leaders urged Wells-Barnett to march at the back of the procession with the other black delegates. But she firmly refused, declaring, "I shall not march at all unless I can march under the Illinois banner."

When the parade started, Wells-Barnett was nowhere to be seen, and the other delegates from Illinois assumed she had given up and joined her black sisters in the back. But as the marchers proceeded down Pennsylvania Avenue, Wells-Barnett slipped out of the crowd of spectators and marched with her state delegation.

Three years later, she proudly led her suffrage club in a parade through Chicago, when 5,000 suffragists marched to the 1916 Republican National Convention to demand the party's support for women's suffrage. When American women finally received the right to vote in 1920, Wells-Barnett urged black women to exercise this right as a means of achieving social and political equality for all African Americans.

7

Riverside, California ❖ 1916

The House on LEMON Street

Like immigrants from Europe, those from Europe from Asia came to America seeking economic opportunities. But they soon found that there were limits placed on what they could achieve in the United States. Asian immigrants were denied U.S. citizenship and all the privileges that status entailed, including the right to own property. In 1916, one family battled against the unjust laws aimed at immigrants of Japanese ancestry. In doing so, they lent their own voices to the growing chorus of Asian Americans insisting: "We belong here."

by **MARIA FLEMING**

The children of Jukichi Harada, a Japanese emigré living in Riverside, California, in the early 1900s, used to tease their father about being more patriotic than any American citizen. He named his restaurant after one of his heroes — George Washington. Portraits of other U.S. presidents lined the walls of the eatery, where Harada served "all-American" food. On the Fourth of July and other national holidays, he proudly displayed an American flag outside his home. Harold Harada, the youngest of Jukichi's six children, describes his father as someone who "oozed red, white and blue."

But the love Jukichi Harada felt for America was not returned by his adopted country. He lived in the United States during a time of deep prejudice against Asian Americans. In the Western states, where most Asian immigrants lived, white citizens formed exclusion leagues whose sole purpose was to keep Chinese, Filipinos, Japanese, Koreans and other Asians out of the U.S.

The offer of American citizenship, extended to tens of thousands of European immigrants, was denied those of Asian descent. Asian Americans couldn't vote, testify in court or practice certain professions. And in almost a dozen Western states, immigrants from Asia didn't even have the right to buy a house or own a farm.

Prejudice against Asians in America hadn't always run so deep. When the first Chinese immigrants arrived in the mid-1800s, railroad companies welcomed them as a cheap and reliable source of labor. But after the railroads were completed, whites found the Chinese competing for factory jobs they wanted for themselves. They pushed for laws banning Chinese immigration; the Chinese Exclusion Act of 1882 became the first U.S. law to bar a particular ethnic group.

Japanese immigrants were the next to arrive from Asia. For the most part, they devoted their energies to agriculture. Japanese laborers drained the swamplands and irrigated the deserts that would become some of the West Coast's most productive fields and orchards. When Japanese immigrants started to become successful farmers themselves, whites again panicked that the prosperity of "outsiders" would diminish their own prospects and profits.

In California, Washington, Oregon, Arizona and other states, legislators enacted laws that said "aliens ineligible to citizenship" could not own land. The laws did not specify Japanese immigrants, but that is whom they targeted. The alien land laws, as they were called, guaranteed that immigrants of Japanese descent would remain field hands and tenant farmers.

The perceived economic threat that Asian Americans presented to U.S. citizens, most of them recent immigrants from Europe themselves, only partially accounted for discrimination against them. The other factor inspiring this resentment was a deep-seated ethnic prejudice. Asian immigrants looked very different from European immigrants. They wore different clothes, ate different foods, practiced different religions. And perhaps most significantly, their skin was a different color.

As a document from one Asian exclusion league pronounced, "The preservation of the Caucasian race upon American soil and particularly upon the Western soil thereof, necessitates the adoption of all possible measures to prevent or minimize the immigration of Asiatics to America."

But despite a different skin color and cultural background, Jukichi Harada had emigrated to

WASHINGTON RESTAURANT

J. HARADA, Proprietor

Open from 5 a.m. to 8 p.m.   Prompt and Courteous Service

DINNER, 15c, and Up

Dinner includes bowl of Soup, and one cup of Coffee, Tea, Milk, or Orange Kola and one order of Dessert.   Chocolate, 5c extra.   Side Dish of Meat or Fish, 10c extra and Up.   Extra orders of Dessert or Milk, 5c extra.

Date..191...

SOUP

FISH

The name and decor of Jukichi Harada's restaurant reflected his strong patriotism.

In 1911, Jukichi and Ken Harada felt optimistic that they would continue to improve the quality of life for their children.

America for the same reasons most Europeans did: He thought he would find better job opportunities in the United States; he also believed his children would experience more freedom growing up in America than they would in what was, at the time, a restrictive, tradition-bound Japanese society.

Although trained as a teacher in Japan, Jukichi worked for several years as a mess cook for a U.S. navy ship, traveling between Japan and the United States. In 1903, at the age of 23, he sailed away from Japan for good and settled in Los Angeles, California. Two years later, he was joined by his wife, Ken, and young son, Masa Atsu, whom he had left behind in Japan. While in Los Angeles, both Jukichi and Ken worked in a cafe, cooking and waiting tables.

In the fall of 1905, they moved south to the booming citrus town of Riverside, where they found jobs in another restaurant. Despite a climate of hostility toward Asian Americans, the Haradas worked hard and prospered. In a few years, they had saved enough to rent and run their own rooming house and open a restaurant.

The rooming house and eatery served mostly the farm hands who picked and packed oranges and lemons from the citrus groves surrounding the city and laborers who worked in the nearby citrus crate factory. The Haradas lived with their boarders on the crowded second floor of the rooming house.

The two businesses required the entire family's efforts. Their days began at 5 a.m., when the restaurant opened to serve breakfast to pickers heading to the citrus groves. Jukichi Harada waited tables and worked the cash register while Ken cooked breakfast, lunch and dinner. The children took care of various tasks, depending on their age. The older siblings washed dishes and mopped floors around their school schedules, while the little ones stood watch at the front door and called out *Okasan!* — "Customer!" — if someone came in while Ken and Jukichi were both working in the kitchen.

At night, after the 15-hour workday, Jukichi would practice *sumi-e*, a form of Japanese calligraphy. He was so skilled with the brushwork that stonecutters

in Riverside would hire him to inscribe tombstones for the Japanese cemetery.

Although the Haradas worked long hours and led a modest life, they were content. Jukichi and Ken Harada felt optimistic that they would continue to improve the quality of life for their children. Of course, the Haradas encountered prejudice, as other Japanese in America did. They learned to avoid the segregated public facilities and ignore occasional verbal insults.

But Jukichi Harada did not feel these slights kept him from fulfilling his ambitions. His only deep regret was that he was unable to become an American citizen, despite his persistent efforts. Jukichi wrote repeatedly to the naval commander in Washington,

Jukichi decided to put the deed to the house in the name of 3-year-old Yoshizo, 5-year-old Sumi, and 9-year-old Mine because they were U.S. citizens by birth. Masa Atsu (at left) was born in Japan.

D.C., asking that he be granted citizenship status in light of his maritime service. Each rebuff was another stinging disappointment.

"I have lived in America now a long time," Harada lamented. "My heart is American. All my sympathies are American. I think American, but the law will not let me become an American."

Jukichi did not let the disappointment of this rejection fester into bitterness. Instead, his children remember, he strove harder to be a model citizen. He was active in the community and generous with his small income. He wanted his children to assimilate into American culture and encouraged them to attain the highest level of education.

Then in 1913, tragedy struck. Ken and Jukichi's five-year-old son, Tadao, contracted diphtheria. He died one autumn day in his father's arms. Jukichi blamed the death on the family's living conditions. The boarding house, filled with laborers from the fields and factories, was crowded and dusty. There was nowhere for the children to

PROPERTY VALUES

AT ISSUE
★ ★ ★

For much of American history, law and custom have created segregated housing patterns.

Beginning in the early 20th century, white communities around the country passed local ordinances that forbade blacks, Jews and some ethnic minorities from buying property in their neighborhoods. Excluded groups were restricted to housing in certain sections of cities and towns — sections that were often already overcrowded and offered inferior housing.

In 1917, the Supreme Court ruled that such ordinances were unconstitutional. But white communities employed other means to ensure residential segregation. One of the most popular methods was the restrictive covenant. The covenants were agreements signed by property owners and real estate

agents in some white neighborhoods promising they would not sell or lease the property to a specified group. Even the Federal Housing Administration endorsed such practices and refused to back loans in communities that admitted "inharmonious" — or non-white — groups.

More than any other group, African Americans were the targets of these discriminatory practices. Around the nation, whites fiercely resisted blacks moving into their neighborhoods. Arson, bombings, cross burnings and threats of physical violence were all used to force black residents out of white neighborhoods. In July of 1951, for example, Illinois Governor Adlai Stevenson declared martial law in Cicero, a suburb of Chicago, when a mob of 4,000 whites rioted for four days to prevent a black man from moving into a white neighborhood. Similar incidents occurred in cities around play outside, which Harada believed deprived them of healthy fresh air. He made immediate plans to improve his family's living situation.

He found what he believed would be the means for safeguarding his family's health and well-being — a simple wooden frame house in the heart of Riverside's downtown residential district. White with gray trim, the house had six rooms, enough to accommodate the growing Harada family. It was also near a good school and the church the family attended. And best of all, the house boasted a small yard out back where his children could play in the fresh air. He made plans to purchase the property.

Jukichi Harada was aware of the Alien Land Law of 1913 — passed just six months before his son's death — that prohibited non-citizens from owning property in California. The logical solution to this problem, he believed, was to put the deed to the house in the name of three of his children: 9-year-old Mine, 5-year-old Sumi, and 3-year-old Yoshizo. Because the children had been born in the U.S., they were citizens by law. Jukichi would act as trustee of the property until the children were old enough to assume ownership.

On his way back from the real estate agent's office, where he had just signed the papers for purchase, Harada bumped into his soon-to-be-next-door neighbor, Cynthia Robinson. Alarmed that a Japanese family would be moving to the all-white block, Robinson quickly spread word through the neighborhood. Within days, several families had organized a committee with the aim of keeping the Haradas from buying the house on Lemon Street.

The committee approached Harada and asked him to give up the property. They offered him $2,000 for the house, which was $500 more than he had paid for it. When he declined the offer, the committee hired a lawyer, who again tried to persuade the Haradas to sell. Jukichi Harada refused the offer even more vehemently, vowing to hold onto, at any cost, the house that would put his children in a better living environment.

"I won't sell," Harada repeated. "You can murder me, you can throw me into the sea, and I won't sell."

The neighborhood confrontation soon attracted the attention of the larger community and, eventually, the state. Politicians and citizens alike were concerned that the Haradas were one of many families finding loopholes in the Alien Land Law. Sixty families signed a petition demanding that the Haradas be evicted from the house on Lemon Street.

the nation, including Miami, Dallas, Nashville, Denver, St. Louis and Detroit.

The National Association for the Advancement of Colored People (NAACP) devoted a great deal of its energy and resources to overturning restrictive covenants and other discriminatory housing practices. In 1948, the NAACP won an important victory when the U.S. Supreme Court declared in *Shelley* v. *Kraemer* that such agreements could not legally be enforced. Twenty years later, in *Jones* v. *Mayer,* the Supreme Court went even further in preventing housing discrimination by ruling that a person could not be denied the opportunity to buy a home on the basis of race. Other laws promoting fair housing were passed in the 1970s and '80s as well.

Although the legal obstacles to achieving integrated housing have been removed, the legacy of these discriminatory practices still defines our communities. Most Americans live, work, worship and attend school with people of their own race. In 2000, *The New York Times* surveyed black and white Americans about racial attitudes. The poll revealed that racial hostility has sharply declined since the Civil Rights Movement. The vast majority of those polled, both black and white, said they had no preference about the racial composition of the neighborhoods. And yet the majority also lived in neighborhoods that were composed almost solely of their own racial group, suggesting that segregated communities may be more a matter of history and habit than of choice.

One of the reasons that whites cited for maintaining segregated housing for much of the 20th century was to protect their property values. In fact, the code of ethics of the National Association of Real Estate Boards in 1924 stated that "A Realtor should never be instrumental in introducing into a neighborhood . . . members of any race or nationality, or any individual whose presence will clearly be detrimental to property values in that neighborhood." Integration, the majority culture believed, had its costs.

But what price have we paid as a nation in maintaining segregated communities? And what values do we need for the 21st century to finally topple the invisible walls that still divide our communities along racial lines?

Today, the house on Lemon Street looks much as it did nearly a century ago, when it first caught Jukichi Harada's eye.

J. C. Hansler, one of the petition's signers and the owner of a downtown furniture shop not far from the Harada house, told a newspaper reporter, "I don't want to have any trouble with Harada and don't want to hurt his feelings, but we feel that if he lives there other Japanese will move in and it will inevitably hurt all the property in the neighborhood."

Other neighbors were even more hostile toward the Haradas. One boy threw rocks at the children. A woman who owned a house on the corner of Lemon Street would shout at the children as they passed, "You Japs stay on your side of the street! Don't you ever walk over here!" Fearing for their children's safety, Ken and Jukichi forbade them from straying beyond their fenced yard.

There were other whites in the community, however, who offered their support to the Haradas. One, Frank Miller, was a prominent businessman. His interest in Japanese art and culture led him to become acquainted with Riverside's Asian American community. When the state eventually filed a lawsuit against Jukichi Harada in October of 1916 in the first test case of California's Alien Land Law, Frank Miller arranged to have his brother, a prominent attorney, defend him.

"Japan vs. America," announced the headline of a *Los Angeles Times* news article covering the lawsuit. This was not a fight between nations, but the wording indicates the symbolic importance of the issue.

The crux of the state's case was that although Jukichi Harada had put the deed of the house in the name of his citizen children, the purchase was actually for his own personal benefit. California Senator Miguel Estudillo explained the state's position. "If, by decision in this case it is found possible for Japanese aliens to purchase and hold property in the name of minor children who are native born there will be no limit to the amount or nature of the property they can purchase, and no stopping their invasion of any district in any community."

But by the time the case came to trial, the Haradas' presence in the neighborhood had already eroded some of the ill will toward them. Neighbors testifying in court seemingly did more to help the Haradas than hurt them. Even Cynthia Robinson, who had organized the neighborhood

Equality Before the Law

The equal protection clause of the 14th Amendment, cited in the Harada ruling, has been used as a weapon in thousands of civil rights battles since its enactment in 1868. The clause holds that no state shall "deny to any person within its jurisdiction the equal protection of the laws." Like the amendment as a whole, this provision was written with ex-slaves in mind, but its language made the question inevitable: Was it broad enough to protect from discrimination other groups who had been pushed to the margins of American society?

Chinese immigrants — the targets of numerous patently discriminatory laws — were among the first minority groups to put the equal protection clause to the test. One such claim that reached the U.S. Supreme Court was brought by a Chinese business owner named Yick Wo, who resided in San Francisco.

Not much is known about the life of Yick Wo. Even his name is the subject of some dispute. We do know that Yick Wo arrived in the United States from China in 1861. He may have been lured by the prospect of mining for gold, or he may have tried to find work on the railroads, like thousands of Chinese who immigrated in the 1800s. Once here, however, they encountered deep prejudice. Laws denied them citizenship and locked them out of certain types of employment. With limited economic opportunities, many Chinese laborers — including Yick Wo — turned to the laundry business.

There, too, they were bombarded with oppressive regulations. One example was a San Francisco ordinance, passed in 1880, that prohibited the operation of a laundry in a wooden building without the consent of the Board of Supervisors.

Yick Wo applied for the renewal of his license in 1885. Although his business had operated in the same location for more than 20 years, and had passed inspections by both the health and fire departments, the Board of Supervisors denied his application.

He may not have been overly surprised. The ordinance was ostensibly a public safety measure, but it became clear that the Board of Supervisors' attention was focused less on the structural composition of the buildings than on the racial composition of the ownership. About 310 of the 320 laundry businesses in the city were housed in wooden buildings. The board denied every one of the approximately 200 applications submitted by Chinese owners, and granted all but one of the approximately 80 submitted by non-Chinese owners.

Despite the denial of his application, Yick Wo continued to operate his business. For doing so, he was arrested, convicted and, upon his nonpayment of the fine imposed, he was imprisoned. He refused to give up, however, and challenged his conviction as a violation of the equal protection clause of the 14th Amendment. His case ultimately came before the U.S. Supreme Court.

Without dissent, the court concluded quite simply that the protections of the 14th Amendment were not "confined to the protection of citizens." Its provisions, the court continued, "are universal in their application to all persons within the territorial jurisdiction, without regard to any differences of race, of color, or of nationality."

Finding no reason for the city's denial of Yick Wo's application other than "hostility to [his] race and nationality," the court ruled the ordinance unconstitutional as applied and Yick Wo's conviction unjustified. The court's broad reading of the applicability of the 14th Amendment would benefit not just Yick Wo, who was ordered released from prison, but others outside the white mainstream who were determined to be included in American society on an equal basis.

committee opposed to the house's sale, testified that the Haradas were "nice people" and kindly, good neighbors.

In September of 1918, San Bernardino Superior Court Judge Hugh H. Craig decided the case in the Haradas' favor. Citing the equal protection clause of the 14th Amendment, he ruled that the Harada children, born in the United States, could not be denied their rights: "They are American citizens, of somewhat humble station, it may be, but still entitled to equal protection of the laws of our land.... The political rights of American citizens are the same, no matter what their parentage."

It was a tremendous victory for the Harada family and an important symbolic victory for other Japanese immigrants trying to make their way in America. Judge Craig's ruling, however, did not dismantle the Alien Land Law. In fact, California passed additional land laws trying — unsuccessfully — to close the loophole of deeding property to citizen children. It would take many more court battles, and many more decades, before the U.S. Supreme Court declared the alien land laws in 10 Western states unconstitutional in 1953.

Jukichi Harada's family would grow and prosper in the house on Lemon Street, but in time they would face a far greater threat to their rights. In 1941 — more than two decades after the Haradas' legal victory — war broke out between the United States and Japan. The Haradas were among the 112,000 Japanese Americans, two-thirds of them U.S. citizens, who were declared enemy aliens and herded into prison camps. Jukichi and Ken Harada were in their 60s at the time and in failing health. Both died behind a barbed wire fence at the Topaz Relocation Center in Utah, 10 months before Pres. Franklin D. Roosevelt announced that the internment camps would close.

After the Japanese American prisoners were released, the Harada children scattered to different parts of the country. Only Jukichi and Ken's youngest daughter, Sumi, returned to the house that her father had fought so hard to keep. Sumi opened the house up to Japanese internees who had returned to find that their own homes had been confiscated by the government and their possessions destroyed during the anti-Japanese war hysteria. Japanese American families used the Harada house as a way station as they worked to rebuild their lives. Sumi herself remained in the house for the next 50 years, until 1998, when, at the age of 86, poor health forced her to move into a nursing home.

Today, the house on Lemon Street looks much as it did nearly a century ago, when it first caught Jukichi Harada's eye and he imagined his family's future within its solid walls. It stands as a silent sentinel to the history of Japanese men and women's struggle to find their place in America.

"We were born and raised in that house, and twice people tried to take it away from us," says Harold Harada. "The house is meaningful to us; it is proof of what we went through."

In 1991, the house was designated a National Historic Landmark. Harold Harada is certain that his father, were he alive today, would be deeply moved to know his home was of historic importance to the nation he loved so much. There are plans to make it into a small museum dedicated to the Japanese immigrant experience and to Jukichi Harada's battle against California's alien land laws. Although most of Ken and Jukichi's children are now deceased, a museum, Harold hopes, will ensure the preservation of the house on Lemon Street — one man's legacy to his family, and one family's legacy to their country.

The Rocky Road Home

The end of internment didn't bring an end to discrimination against Japanese Americans. Communities that had rejected Japanese immigrants before the war were in no hurry to embrace internees after their release. After enduring two and a half years of hardship and indignity in the prison camps, some Japanese Americans returned to find their homes burned, their farms in ruins and their possessions gone. The unwelcome former residents were harassed, threatened, even shot at.

Fearful that returning evacuees would try to restart their lives in Oregon, that state's legislature passed an Alien Land Law in 1945 that prohibited Japanese Americans not only from owning land but from operating farm equipment. Anti-Japanese sentiment was particularly virulent in Oregon's Hood River Valley. Following the internees' release, hundreds of valley residents signed full-page newspaper ads stating, "So Sorry! Japs Are Not Wanted in Hood River" and "We should never be satisfied until every last Jap has been run out of these United States."

Japanese families faced a host of other obstacles, too. Stores wouldn't sell them groceries. Barbers refused to cut their hair. Produce distributors declined to sell apples and pears from Japanese orchards. Neighbors shunned them. Children were tormented in school. In a particularly hurtful act, the American Legion removed from a war memorial at the county courthouse the names of Japanese Americans fighting in the U.S. armed forces.

But not every voice in Hood River was one of hatred and rejection. Some voices rose above the clamor of intolerance to offer words of consolation and welcome. Members of the Hood River County League for Liberty and Justice were among those who recognized "the grave injustice" done to Japanese Americans and offered their help to returning families.

The league began an education program to dispel myths about the Japanese and urged local ministers to preach tolerance from their pulpits. League members wrote letters to grocery and department stores and tried to convince them to sell to Japanese customers. They drove produce trucks to help Japanese farmers transport their fruits and vegetables to market. One elderly member of the League for Liberty and Justice was known to march into stores that displayed anti-Japanese signs and shame owners into taking them down.

But it was the small gestures that often meant the most to Japanese Americans. One of the first evacuees returning to Hood River after internment remembers walking into a downtown bank. He was met by sneers and icy stares until one teller, with tears in her eyes, rushed from her booth to shake his hand and welcome him home.

Such actions had repercussions. That particular teller was shunned by her co-workers and forced to quit her job. Others were labeled "Jap-lovers" and treated as hostilely as the returning internees. However, these individuals remained committed to reminding Hood River residents of our nation's highest principles.

In the following letter — sent to Japanese Americans upon their return to Hood River — members of the League for Liberty and Justice express their sympathy and support for their Japanese neighbors.

We want you folks to know that there is a group of fair-minded people in the city and valley who have watched with growing resentment and concern, the injustices to which you have been subjected the past few months.

We were probably shocked as much as you were by unreasonable prejudice and vicious actions of certain individuals, and we feel a sense of shame that anything like this could happen in America.

We have organized a group specifically for the purpose of assisting you . . . and our numbers are steadily growing. . . . Already our influence is being felt, and when ordinarily fair-minded people recover a bit from this war hysteria, they will reconsider their present decisions. . . .

Please accept our deepest sympathy and understanding in your present trouble. It is a shameful, unjust and unnecessary ordeal, but we firmly believe that out of it (a trial by fire, as it were) will emerge a better understanding and deeper friendship than we have ever experienced before.

If you should need any help, don't hesitate to call on us. This is the purpose of our organization. We would like to do something, even if it is all too little, to offset some of the wrongs you have endured.

Very sincerely,
Hood River County League for Liberty and Justice
Hazel V. Smith, sec

8

Westminster, California ❧ 1945

A Tale OF
TWO SCHOOLS

Many groups have experienced, and fought against, the indignities of segregation in the United States. In the early 1900s in California and the Southwest, Mexican Americans, or Chicanos, were excluded from "Whites Only" theaters, parks, swimming pools, restaurants — even schools. Immigrants from Mexico waged many battles against such discriminatory treatment, often risking their jobs in fields and factories and enduring threats of deportation. In 1945, one couple in California won a significant victory in their struggle to secure the best education for thousands of Chicano children.

by MARIA FLEMING

In the fall of 1944, Soledad Vidaurri took her children and those of her brother, Gonzalo Méndez, to enroll at the 17th Street School in Westminster, California. Although they were cousins and shared a Mexican heritage, the Méndez and Vidaurri children looked quite different: Sylvia, Gonzalo Jr. and Geronimo Méndez had dark skin, hair and eyes, while Alice and Virginia Vidaurri had fair complexions and features.

An administrator looked the five children over. Alice and Virginia could stay, he said. But their dark-skinned cousins would have to register at the Hoover School, the town's "Mexican school" located a few blocks away. Furious at such blatant discrimination, Vidaurri returned home without registering any of the children in either school.

In the 1940s, Westminster was a small farming community in the southern part of the state. Lush citrus groves, lima bean fields and sugar beet farms stretched in every direction from a modest downtown business district. Most of the men and women working in those fields were first- and second-generation immigrants from Mexico who were employed by white ranchers.

Like many California towns at the time, Westminster really comprised two separate worlds: one Anglo, one Mexican. While Anglo growers welcomed Chicano workers in their fields during times of economic prosperity, they shut them out of mainstream society. Most people of Mexican ancestry lived in *colonias* — segregated residential communities — on the fringes of Anglo neighborhoods. The housing was often substandard, with inadequate plumbing and often no heating. Roads were unpaved and dusty.

Westminster's Hoover School was in the heart of one such *colonia* and was attended by the children of Mexican field laborers. A small frame building at the edge of a muddy cow pasture, the Hoover School stood in stark contrast to the sleek 17th Street School, with its handsome green lawns and playing fields.

The Westminster School District was not alone in discriminating against Chicano students. At the time, more than 80 percent of school districts in California with large Mexican populations practiced segregation. The segregation of Chicano children was also widespread in Texas, New Mexico and Arizona.

The Mexican schools were typically housed in run-down buildings. They employed less-experienced teachers than the Anglo schools. Chicano children were given shabbier books and equipment than their white peers and were taught in more crowded classrooms. Perhaps the greatest difference between the schools, however, was in their curricula. While geometry and biology were taught at the Anglo schools, classes at the Mexican schools focused on teaching boys industrial skills and girls domestic tasks.

Many Anglo educators did not expect, or encourage, Chicano students to advance beyond the 8th grade. Instead, the curriculum at the Mexican schools was designed, as one district superintendent put it, "to help these children take their place in society."

That "place" was the lowest rung of the economic ladder, providing cheap, flexible labor for the prospering agricultural communities of California and the Southwest. At the time, more than 80 percent of the agricultural labor force in southern California was Mexican. An advanced education would only make Mexican Americans dissatisfied with farm labor, some white educators reasoned. As one school superintendent in Texas told his fellow educators, "You have doubtless heard that ignorance is bliss; it seems that it is so when one has to transplant onions.... If a man has very much sense or education either, he is not going to stick to this kind of work. So you see it is up to the white population to keep the Mexican on his knees in an onion patch."

But Chicano men and women had different ideas about their children's futures. Like other immigrant groups, Chicano field laborers believed that education was the ticket to a better life in America, a way out of the heat and dust of the fields.

Gonzalo and Felícitas Méndez knew well the difficult life of field laborers. Both had emigrated to the United States as young children. Like thousands of Mexicans in the early 20th century, Gonzalo's family had fled political turmoil in their native country. They left behind a successful ranch in Chihuahua and found jobs as day laborers in the citrus groves of Southern California.

Felícitas Gomez had emigrated to America from Juncos, Puerto Rico, when she was 10. The Gomez family led a migrant life, following the harvest from Texas to Arizona to California. Eventually, they settled in the southern California *colonia* where the Méndezes lived, and in 1936, Felícitas and Gonzalo married.

By that time, Gonzalo had a reputation in the county as a champion orange picker, and he commanded a slightly higher wage than other field workers. Felícitas, thrifty and resourceful, saved what she could from Gonzalo's wages, and in a few years the couple were able to lease their own ranch — 40 acres of asparagus in the town of Westminster.

The Méndezes were among the few Chicano tenant farmers in Orange County. Most Latinos at the time held low-paying jobs as field workers. Employment opportunities for Mexican Americans were severely limited. Discrimination prevented them from getting jobs in restaurants, department

---

(Left) Through the labors of migrant workers, California's agricultural business flourished and growers prospered. *(Below)* Chicano workers lived in small shacks without plumbing or heating, usually on the outskirts of town.

(Top) Because their skin was dark, Sylvia, Geronimo and Gonzalo Méndez (shown here with a baby sitter) were assigned to an inferior school. (Above) Their Vidaurri cousins Alice (at left) and Virginia were assigned to the Anglo school. Edward Vidaurri (center) missed the opening of school because of illness.

stores and even many factories, making it extremely difficult for them to advance economically.

Both Felícitas and Gonzalo had been forced to abandon their education in grade school in order to support their families. But they had higher hopes for young Sylvia, Gonzalo Jr. and Geronimo. And when Soledad Vidaurri told her brother and sister-in-law that their children had been refused admission to the 17th Street School because they — unlike her own children — didn't look "White enough," Gonzalo and Felícitas were outraged.

"How could it be possible?" they wondered. They were American citizens. Gonzalo had been naturalized just a few years before; and because Felícitas

had been born in a U.S. territory, she was a citizen by birth. Both thought of themselves as Americans and told their children they were Americans.

Not that they were unfamiliar with the prejudice toward Latinos, however. For people of Mexican descent living in California and the Southwest, discrimination was part of the social landscape. Many parks, hotels, dance halls, stores, eateries and barbershops were off limits. Mexican Americans were forced to sit in the balcony in movie theaters. In many communities, they were only permitted to swim one day a week at the public pool, just before it was cleaned and drained.

The fact that the Méndezes were fairly prosperous tenant farmers did not make them any more acceptable to the mainstream community. They were used to being told in restaurants, "We don't serve Mexicans here," and being informed by store clerks that they would have to wait to make their purchases until all the white customers had been served.

"That's when you learned to walk away," Felícitas later remembered.

But this time, Gonzalo and Felícitas Méndez didn't plan to walk away. They were ready to do battle with the Westminster School District for the sake of their children's education. Realizing that other Chicano families in the community faced the same problem, the Méndezes organized a group of Mexican parents to protest the segregation of their children in the shabbier school. Together, they sent a letter to the board of education demanding that the schools be integrated. Their request was flatly denied.

Gonzalo continued to petition school district administrators. Worn down by his persistence, the school superintendent finally agreed to make an exception for the Méndez children and admit them to the Anglo school. But the Méndezes immediately rejected his offer. The school would have to admit all of the Chicano children in the community or none of them.

The Méndezes hired a civil rights attorney, David Marcus, who had recently won a lawsuit on behalf of Mexican Americans in nearby San Bernardino seeking to integrate the public parks and pools. The Méndezes also learned that parents in other school districts had been fighting against segregation, too. Marcus suggested that they join forces, and on March 2, 1945, the Méndezes and four other

Mexican American families filed a class action suit against the Westminster, Garden Grove, El Modena and Santa Ana boards of education on behalf of 5,000 Mexican American children attending segregated, inferior schools.

The Méndezes threw themselves into the trial preparations. Gonzalo took a year off from work to organize Latino men and women and gather evidence for the case. Every day, he and David Marcus drove across Orange County's patchwork of vegetable farms and citrus groves, stopping in the *colonias*. They knocked on doors and tried to convince Mexican American parents and their children to testify in court.

It was no easy task. Some workers feared that their Anglo bosses might fire them if they testified. Or worse, they might be deported. But slowly, the plaintiffs built their case. Gonzalo offered to pay the

Segregation in the Far North

In the spring of 1944, seventeen-year-old Alberta Schenck walked into the Alaska Dream Theatre in Nome and took a seat in the "Whites Only" section. When the manager asked her to move, Schenck, whose mother was Eskimo and whose father was white, refused. The manager then called the chief of police, who forcibly ejected the teenager from the theater and arrested her. Schenck spent the night in Nome's city jail.

It wasn't the first time Alberta Schenck had protested discrimination against Alaska's Native peoples. In fact, she had voiced her disapproval of the theater's policy just a few weeks earlier. Schenck was then employed as an usher at the theater after school. But every time she directed a Native moviegoer to the segregated balcony she felt humiliated for both herself and the customer. When Schenck finally complained to the manager about the policy, she was fired. Later, she wrote a letter to the editor of the *Nome Nugget* in which she described the pain and injustice of segregation.

"What has hurt us constantly," Schenck wrote, "is that we are not able to go to a public theater and sit where we wish, but yet we pay the SAME price as anyone else and our money is GLADLY received."

Throughout the territory, Native peoples faced similar discrimination. So pervasive was segregation in Alaska that a reporter visiting the territory in 1943 observed that the social position of Native peoples seemed "equivalent to that of a Negro in Georgia or Mississippi."

But Schenck had staged her one-woman protest at a time when Alaska's Native peoples were beginning to organize politically and demand fair treatment. Native activists had an important ally in their struggle: Ernest Gruening, the governor of the Alaska Territory. In 1943, Gruening had submitted a bill to the territory's legislature calling for an end to the segregation of Alaska's Native peoples in public facilities. However, the bill was defeated.

The day after her arrest, Alberta Schenck sent a telegram to Gruening describing her experience at the Dream Theatre. The governor wrote Schenck back, vowing to re-introduce the bill during the next legislative session. "[I]f it becomes law," Gruening wrote, "you may be certain that the unpleasant experience which has been yours will not happen again to anyone in Alaska. It should never have happened — in America."

The governor kept his promise. This time, the measure passed. On February 16, 1945, Gov. Gruening signed the bill into law, officially guaranteeing "full and equal accommodations, facilities and privileges to all citizens" of the Alaska Territory.

(Left) Pickers followed the ripening of the fruit from grove to grove. (Below right) As the flow of Mexican immigrants into the U.S. increased in the early 1900s, so did racist attitudes in Anglo communities.

transportation costs and lost wages of anyone willing to travel to Los Angeles and appear in court during the trial.

Meanwhile, Felícitas took over the daily operation of the farm. In the little spare time she had, she organized a group of local Latino parents to support the five plaintiffs in the lawsuit.

Finally, the trial date arrived. Now it was up to the courts to decide if the Latino men and women who had helped California's agricultural economy grow and thrive were entitled to the same rights as those who prospered from their labor.

During the trial, defense attorney Joel Ogle pointed out that the 1896 Supreme Court decision in *Plessy* v. *Ferguson* had given legal sanction to racial segregation, provided that the separate facilities for different races were equal. Furthermore, Ogle maintained, there were sound educational and social advantages to segregated schooling. The "Mexican schools" gave special instruction to students who didn't speak English and who were unfamiliar with American values and customs. Such "Americanization" programs benefited both Anglos and Mexicans, Ogle argued.

But this educational rationalization for segregation was undermined by the testimony of 9-year-old Sylvia, 8-year-old Gonzalo and 7-year-old Geronimo Méndez. All spoke fluent English, as did

many of the other children who attended the Hoover School. In fact, further testimony revealed that no language proficiency tests had even been given to Chicano students. Rather, enrollment decisions were based entirely on last names and skin color, as evidenced by the experience of the Méndez children and their cousins.

The racist underpinnings of such "Americanization" programs became apparent when James L. Kent, the superintendent of the Garden Grove School District, took the stand. Under oath, Kent said that he believed that people of Mexican descent were intellectually, culturally and morally inferior to European Americans. Even if a Latino child had the same academic qualifications as a white child, Kent stated, he would never allow that child to enroll in an Anglo school.

It was testimony that made the Latino men and women who had gathered in the courtroom to show their support for the suit wince in pain — and anger. Felícitas said later that she never forgot Kent's hate-laced testimony.

"He said Mexicans should be segregated like pigs in pigpens," she recalled. "He said Mexicans were filthy and had lice and all kinds of diseases."

U.S. District Court Judge Paul J. McCormick was also appalled by Kent's blatant bigotry. On February 18, 1946, he ruled in favor of the plaintiffs. In his opinion, McCormick pointed out that segregation "fosters antagonisms in the children and suggests inferiority among them where none exists." Because the separate schools created social inequality, he reasoned, they were in violation of the students' constitutional rights. He also pointed out that there was no sound educational basis for the segregation of Anglo and Mexican students since research showed that segregation worked against language acquisition and cultural assimilation.

The Orange County school boards filed an appeal.

But dramatic social change was occurring on a national level following World War II, and Orange County school officials would find their position on segregation coming under increasing attack. After fighting for democracy abroad, Mexican American soldiers balked against the rigid lines of division when they returned home. "How could America declare itself the leader of the free world, while it trampled the rights of its own citizens?" they asked. Latino veterans formed civil rights groups and demanded change. Around the country, other minority groups were waging similar battles.

By now, the Méndez lawsuit had drawn national attention. Civil rights lawyers in other states were watching the proceedings closely. For half a century, they had been trying to strike down the "separate but equal" doctrine of *Plessy* v. *Ferguson*, and they thought that *Méndez* just might be the test case to do it.

Among those following the suit was a young African-American attorney named Thurgood Marshall. Marshall and two of his colleagues from the National Association for the Advancement of Colored People (NAACP) submitted an *amicus curiae* — "friend of the court" — brief in the appellate case. Among the other groups submitting *amicus* briefs were the League of United Latin American Citizens, the Japanese American Citizens League and the Jewish Congress.

Bilingual Education, Circa 1920

DOCUMENT

World War I set off an intense wave of anti-immigrant hysteria. Then, as now, bilingual education was a contentious issue. Immigrants and their allies challenged laws that called for English-only instruction. Teachers were arrested in Iowa, Nebraska and Ohio for violating such laws. In 1923, the Supreme Court ruled that these laws, which existed in more than 20 states, were unconstitutional. Following is a reaction to that ruling that appeared in Onze Toekomst, a Dutch-language newspaper.

The opinion of the Supreme Court finally gives the right to different religious organizations and individuals to teach religion and other subjects in languages other than English. This means that we can now instruct in the lower schools in all the courses in Dutch or German or Polish or any other language. A courageous decision! Hurrah for American liberty! May she live long.

We are not for Dutch schools exclusively. That would not only be impossible, but it would be a crime against our children. It would be ungrateful to the land. It would be unpatriotic and therefore the American language should be first in our lower schools . . . [The Dutch] want to be good Americans. They do not want to separate themselves from the nation. Instead, they want to share their gifts and blessings with the nation. But we will not throw our children head over heels into the maelstrom. The Dutch want their children to be as themselves and to maintain a spiritual tie with their ancestors. . . . In order to do this, they need as an instrument their own language.

On April 14, 1947, the Ninth Circuit Court of Appeals in San Francisco upheld the lower court decision. The court stopped short, however, of condemning the "separate but equal" doctrine of *Plessy v. Ferguson*. The NAACP and other groups eagerly waited for Orange County school officials to file an appeal that would bring the case before the U.S. Supreme Court. But lawyers for the school read the writing on the wall: Mainstream public opinion had shifted, and the era of segregation was coming to a close. The defense decided not to appeal the decision further. An opportunity to overturn *Plessy* would have to wait.

Even if it would not rewrite the law of the land, *Méndez* v. *Westminster* still had a significant regional impact. Like a pebble tossed into a pond, the legal victory sent ripples of change throughout the Southwest. In more than a dozen communities in California alone, Mexican Americans filed similar lawsuits. Chicano parents sought and won representation on school boards and gained a voice in their children's education. The decision also prompted California Governor Earl Warren to sign legislation repealing a state law that called for the segregation of American Indian and Asian American students.

Seven years later, the NAACP did find a successful test case to reverse *Plessy v. Ferguson*. Thurgood Marshall argued the landmark *Brown v. Board of Education of Topeka* before the U.S. Supreme Court, presenting the same social science and human rights theories he had outlined in his *amicus curiae* brief for the *Méndez* case. Former California Governor Earl Warren, who had been appointed chief justice of the U.S. Supreme Court, wrote the historic opinion that finally ended the legal segregation of students on the basis of race in American schools in 1954.

AN EDUCATION IN CITIZENSHIP

DOCUMENT

The amicus curiae *brief submitted in the Méndez suit by Thurgood Marshall and his colleagues at the NAACP argued that segregation harmed all Americans, not just the targets of discrimination.*

The segregated citizen cannot give his full allegiance to a system of law and justice based on the proposition that "all men are created equal" when the community denies that equality by compelling his children to attend separate schools. Nor can the white child learn this fundamental of American citizenship when his community sets a contradictory example.

Educational segregation creates still another barrier to American citizenship. It promotes racial strife by teaching the children of both the dominant and minority groups to regard each other as something different and apart. And one of the great lessons of human history is that man tends to fear and hate that which he feels is alien.

It is essential for the successful development of our country as a nation of free people that the sympathies and tolerance which we wish practiced in later life be fostered in the classroom.

In September of 1947, Sylvia, Gonzalo Jr. and Geronimo Méndez enrolled at the 17th Street School in Westminster without incident. Integrated schools also opened that fall in Garden Grove, El Modena and Santa Ana. Felícitas and Gonzalo Méndez quietly resumed their work. At the time, neither really considered the full impact of their legal victory; they were content just to have righted a wrong in their community and to have protected their children's future. In 1964, Gonzalo Méndez died of heart failure. Felícitas continued to live in Southern California until her death in 1998.

Sadly, neither *Méndez* v. *Westminster* nor *Brown v. Board of Education* led to the complete integration of American schools. The long legacy of segregation has left its mark on our current educational system, and integration and equity are issues that schools are still grappling with today. In Santa Ana, California — one of the districts named in the *Méndez* desegregation lawsuit more than 50 years ago — a new school opened in 2000 honoring Gonzalo and Felícitas Méndez, two civil rights pioneers in the continuing struggle to provide equal educational opportunities for all of America's children. ▣

A War on Two Fronts

World War II had a dramatic impact on intergroup relations in the United States. Mexican Americans, Native Americans, Japanese Americans, African Americans and other groups who faced discrimination joined the war effort in large numbers. But unlike white enlistees, members of racial and ethnic minorities believed they were fighting two "wars" — one overseas and one at home.

The rallying cry for African Americans during the war became "Double V" — victory abroad over fascism and in the U.S. over racial inequality. A million African Americans served during the conflict, mostly in segregated units. The black press, the National Association for the Advancement of Colored People, and other civil rights advocates pointed out the hypocrisy of separating troops by race while fighting against Hitler's doctrine of racial supremacy.

As black columnist George Schuyler noted, "Our war is not against Hitler in Europe, but against Hitler in America. Our war is not to defend democracy, but to get a democracy we have never had."

Nearly half a million Mexican Americans served in World War II. Like African Americans, Chicanos fought a war on two fronts. Celebrated for their bravery overseas, Mexican American soldiers found they often couldn't even get a cup of coffee in cafes back home.

Some Mexican American soldiers questioned why they were laying down their lives for a country that treated them like second-class citizens. One Chicano soldier heading for the European frontlines reflected, "I remembered about us, the Mexican Americans . . . how the Anglo had pushed and held back our people in the Southwest. . . . Why fight for America when you have not been treated as an American?" Because it was his home, the soldier decided. "All we wanted was a chance to prove how loyal and American we were." During the war, many Chicanos adopted the slogan "Americans All" to symbolize both their commitment to their country and their hope for a more inclusive society.

For many Japanese Americans, putting on a military uniform was also a way of proving their loyalty to America — a country that had deemed them enemy aliens and incarcerated them in prison camps when the war broke out. Some 33,000 men and women of Japanese descent served during World War II.

Despite — and perhaps because of — their own history of genocide and cultural annihilation in the United States, Native Americans joined the war effort at a higher rate than the general population did, with 25,000 enlisting to serve. Like other members of racial and ethnic minorities, they hoped fighting abroad would gain them respect at home.

Both during and after the war, the beginnings of tremendous social change were evident in the United States. Responding to pressure from black civil rights activists, President Franklin Roosevelt issued an executive order in 1941 banning racial discrimination in defense industries; seven years later, President Harry Truman called for full integration of the military.

One year after the war ended, Truman appointed an interracial civil rights committee, which recommended that Congress pass anti-lynching laws, protect black voting rights and outlaw racial discrimination in all employment. In addition, some of the discriminatory laws barring immigration by Asians and denying them naturalization were finally repealed. The Supreme Court also became more willing to hear civil rights cases in the postwar years.

But perhaps the greatest change had occurred internally, in minority service men and women returning from the war. They had just risked their lives fighting for freedom from oppression abroad. They would accept no less at home. These men and women were now more determined than ever to make America live up to its creed of equality and justice for all. Their experiences during World War II helped pave the way for a civil rights revolution that would transform American society in the second half of the 20th century.

9

Frank's Landing, Washington ✦ 1974

AGAINST THE CURRENT

Between 1789 and 1871, the U.S. government made 371 treaties with Indian nations. To Native peoples, these were — and still are — sacred agreements. The treaties often involved the surrender of land in exchange for certain protections by the federal government. But time and time again, the United States violated the agreements, trampling Indian rights. Native peoples have constantly struggled to make the U.S. government honor its treaty obligations, often without success.

For generations, Indians in the Pacific Northwest were locked in a battle with state agencies over the tribes' treaty fishing rights. In the 1960s and '70s, that battle turned into a full-scale war during a series of confrontations on Northwest rivers and streams as Native peoples fought to protect not just their livelihoods but their traditional way of life.

by BETH HEGE PIATOTE

One day in 1945, a 14-year-old Nisqually Indian boy named Billy Frank Jr. went to his favorite fishing spot at the mouth of the river that ran past his home in western Washington. The place was called "Frank's Landing" after his family, and he had fished there many times.

Also on the river that day were state game wardens. But it wasn't fish the wardens were looking to catch. It was Indians.

The state officials were arresting Native Americans for fishing, despite their treaty rights to do so. The state claimed that treaties made 100 years earlier between Native peoples and the U.S. government only protected the tribes' rights to fish on their reservations. But since the Nisqually reservation had been taken over by the U.S. Army to build a fort during World War II, the Nisqually had no choice but to seek other fishing areas. The Nisqually people believed that their forced removal shouldn't mean an end to their treaty rights to fish.

Billy Frank had walked out of his house that day into the middle of a conflict that would last 30 years. Despite his age, Frank was hauled off to jail like every other tribal fisher at Frank's Landing.

During the next three decades, he and dozens of other Northwest Indians would be arrested many more times. They would face endless harassment, threats, racist attacks, loss of property and even violence. They would spend thousands of dollars on bail, fines and attorney's fees. And eventually, after years of fighting against a strong current of prejudice and misunderstanding that threatened their very survival, Northwest Native peoples and their rights would see a new day.

The fishing rights conflict between the tribes and the state governments of Washington and Oregon actually began many years before Billy Frank Jr. was arrested for the first time — years before he was even born. The controversy was part of a larger history dating back to the time when the region's indigenous peoples first made canoes and fished freely in their homeland.

Billy Frank — like all Northwest Indians — belongs to a long tradition that sees fishing as central to existence. In fact, most Northwest tribes call themselves "salmon people" for their particular relationship to the fish. In their belief system, salmon

(Left) In the belief systems of Northwest tribes, salmon are sacred. *(Above)* Native fishermen sometimes construct fishing platforms on the banks of salmon rivers.

are sacred, a source of spiritual strength as well as physical nourishment. Native cosmology is full of images of fish — revealed in art, ceremony and traditional stories that link the salmon and human behavior. Northwest Native peoples have old traditions that are still carried out today to honor and protect the salmon.

Before white settlers arrived in the Northwest, Native fishers relied on nets, fishing weirs (special nets set in rivers and streams), traps and spears to capture salmon. Over-fishing was never a problem, partly because the technology didn't allow it, and partly because it was impractical for the semi-nomadic lifestyle of the Northwest people. In addition, it was generally not a cultural value to over-consume, particularly a sacred creature like the salmon.

The lives of the Native people and the salmon changed dramatically when white settlers, lured

by the U.S. government's promises of "free" land for homesteaders, streamed into the Northwest during the mid-19th century. Isaac Stevens, appointed governor of the Washington Territory and superintendent of Indian affairs, was charged with negotiating treaties with the Native nations, overseeing the settlement of the area by whites and completing a survey of the land for potential railway routes.

The treaty-making process between Stevens and the Indians was flawed in several ways. First, the Native nations did not operate with a centralized form of government. Stevens addressed this problem by simply appointing "chiefs" to sign for their people, a move unpopular among some tribal members who then refused to participate in any talks. Another challenge was finding a common language in which to negotiate. The Chinook language, a trade language of only about 500 words, was used in the negotiations. The combination of limited vocabulary and huge cultural differences between Native and white concepts of ownership left much to be desired in a meeting of equal nations.

Even so, Stevens was able to deliver six major treaties in as many months, which covered the western half of the state and involved some 6,000 Native communities. Through these agreements, the tribes lost millions of acres of land. But the treaties did reserve Northwest Indians' right to fish, which was central to their culture. In treaties penned between December 1854 and July 1855, the language guaranteed the Native people "The right of taking fish at usual and accustomed grounds and stations . . . in common with all citizens of the United States."

At that time, the Indians fished for both their own subsistence and for commerce with the non-Native settlers, and it was understood that this commercial enterprise would be protected. As he presented the treaties, Stevens himself promised: "This paper secures your fish."

But a problem arose that perhaps no one at the treaty signings could have anticipated: the depletion of fish runs. The first decline of the salmon runs began just a decade after the treaties were signed, with the establishment of canneries in the Northwest. Over the next 100 years, other forces threatened the salmon: commercial over-fishing, an explosion of sports fishing, the damming of rivers for electrical power, destructive logging practices and pollution. Some salmon species became extinct.

The scarcity of fish became the driving force behind a grueling succession of legal battles between Natives and whites as they found themselves competing for a dwindling resource.

The earliest settlement of a fishing dispute in court occurred in 1887, when the Yakama Indians challenged a homesteader named Frank Taylor for building a fence along the Columbia River that blocked the Yakamas' access to fish in a "usual and accustomed" place. The Washington Territory court ruled in favor of the Yakamas and ordered the fence to be removed.

During the next century, Natives would see the scales of justice tip back and forth like a seesaw. Several cases that followed the Yakama ruling would deal severe blows to Native interests. In a devastating Washington Supreme Court decision in 1916, a judge ignored the binding agreement of treaties, saying that the court considered Native people "incompetent occupants" of the land, and that "the

> Before long, the state's jails would be filled with Indians who chose civil disobedience as a path to justice.

Indian was a child, and a dangerous child of nature, to be both protected and restrained. In his nomadic life, he was to be left, as long as civilization did not demand his region. When it did demand his region, he was to be allotted a more confined area. . . . These arrangements [the treaties] were but an announcement of our benevolence." Thus, the judge concluded, the Indians had no legal standing.

Other court cases in the early half of the 20th century tried to balance fishing resources among Native, commercial and sport fishing interests. The courts gradually granted states the right to regulate fishing in the form of requiring licenses.

But Native peoples challenged these provisions; their fishing rights, they argued, had been assured by the U.S. government in exchange for vast tracts of land. State governments did not have the power to restrict these federal guarantees.

The U.S. Supreme Court supported this argument in 1941, when it overturned a state court ruling that convicted a Yakama man of fishing without a license.

(*Far left*) Nisqually Chief Leschi led a brief, unsuccessful uprising against Governor Stevens in 1855–56. (*Left*) As governor of the Washington Territory, Isaac Stevens oversaw the negotiation of treaties with the Native nations.

The justices ruled that the state could not require Indians with treaty rights to abide by state regulations except for the purpose of conservation. But this ruling was widely ignored by state fish and game authorities, and they began to arrest tribal fishers who didn't have licenses. It was precisely this issue that landed 14-year-old Billy Frank in jail in 1945. Before long, the state's jails would be filled with Indians who chose civil disobedience as a path to justice.

As questions of regulation went back and forth in the courts over the next 20 years, the frontlines of the fishing rights battle shifted to the rivers and streams of Washington and Oregon. Inspired by the "sit-ins" organized by African Americans in the 1950s and '60s to end segregation in the South, Native Americans in the Pacific Northwest began to organize "fish-ins" along the rivers of the Puget Sound. They defied state regulations and continued to fish in their "usual and accustomed" places, determined to exercise their treaty rights.

State game wardens were equally determined to stop them. They organized stakeouts to catch Indians violating fishing regulations. State agents

THE "DISCOVERY" OF ALCATRAZ

DOCUMENT

The 1960s and '70s ushered in a new wave of American Indian activism. Riding this wave, a group of Indian college students in California and urban Indians in the San Francisco Bay area took over Alcatraz Island for 19 months, symbolically claiming it for Native peoples. Their goal was to draw attention to a long history of government abuses, including land seizures, broken treaties and cultural genocide. In a pointed jab at four centuries of racist U.S. Indian policies, the protesters issued the following sarcasm-laced proclamation "to the Great White Father and All His People."

We, the native Americans, re-claim the land known as Alcatraz Island in the name of all American Indians by right of discovery.

We wish to be fair and honorable in our dealings with the Caucasian inhabitants of the land, and hereby offer the following treaty:

We will purchase said Alcatraz Island for twenty-four (24) dollars in glass beads and red cloth, a precedent set by the white man's purchase of a similar island about 300 years ago. . . .

We will give to the inhabitants of this island a portion of the land for their own to be held in trust by the American

Indian Affairs and by the bureau of Caucasian Affairs to hold in perpetuity — for as long as the sun shall rise and the rivers go down to the sea.

We will further guide the inhabitants in the proper way of living. We will offer them our religion, our education, our life-ways, in order to help them achieve our level of civilization and thus raise them and all their white brothers up from their savage and unhappy state. . . .

We feel that this so-called Alcatraz Island is more than suitable for an Indian reservation, as determined by the white man's own standards. By this we mean that this place resembles most Indian reservations in that:

1. It is isolated from modern facilities, and without adequate means of transportation.
2. It has no fresh running water.
3. It has inadequate sanitation facilities.
4. There are no oil or mineral rights.
5. There is no industry and so unemployment is very great.
6. There are no health care facilities.
7. The soil is rocky and non-productive; and the land does not support game.
8. There are no educational facilities.
9. The population has always exceeded the land base.
10. The population has always been held as prisoners and kept dependent upon others.

Further, it would be fitting and symbolic that ships from all over the world, entering the Golden Gate, would first see Indian Land, and thus be reminded of the true history of the great lands once ruled by free and noble Indians.

(Left) The violent confrontation on the Puyallup River marked a crucial turning point in the fishing wars. (Right) To protect themselves, Indians organized an armed guard around the camp.

hid behind bushes and ambushed Indians as soon as they dropped their nets in the water. Sometimes dozens of officers descended on a handful of Indians, roughing them up before making arrests.

Many of the demonstrations took place at Frank's Landing on the Nisqually River. "They [state officials] watched us 24 hours a day," Billy Frank later recalled. "They confiscated every boat and net we had. We always made our nets, and we just kept making more. We were always ready to make more, to go back to jail." Frank's own traditional dugout canoe, a prized family possession, was seized during one skirmish on the water.

Sometimes the encounters turned violent. One night, a fight broke out between 27 Indians staging a fish-in and 80 game officials — wielding nightsticks and blackjacks — who had come to stop it. Two children nearly drowned during the battle when game wardens capsized the canoe they were in.

As news of the protests spread, members of Indian activist groups around the country joined the fish-ins and provided some much-needed financial aid. Non-Indian sympathizers also came to lend their support. The involvement of celebrities such as actors Marlon Brando and Jane Fonda and social activist and comedian Dick Gregory attracted even

POWER SHIFT

During the last two centuries, the U.S. government has imposed a series of disastrous and often contradictory policies on American Indian tribes. Despite strong Native opposition to each new plan, the policies were deemed to be in the tribes' best interest. Most of these policies eroded tribal land bases, cultures and sovereign powers, and the U.S. government ultimately acknowledged them as failures.

In the 1960s and '70s, Indian activists insisted that Native peoples be given a greater measure of control in shaping and administering federal policies and programs that directly affect their lives. Congress answered their demands by passing the Indian Self-Determination and Education Assistance Act in 1975.

The Congress hereby recognizes the obligation of the United States to respond to the strong expression of the Indian people for self-determination by assuring maximum Indian participation in the direction of educational as well as other Federal services to Indian communities so as to render such services more responsive to the needs and desires of those communities.

The Congress declares its commitment to the maintenance of the Federal Government's unique and continuing relationship with and responsibility to the Indian people through the establishment of a meaningful Indian self-determination policy which will permit an orderly transition from Federal domination of programs for and services to Indians to effective and meaningful participation by the Indian people in the planning, conduct, and administration of those programs and services.

DOCUMENT

greater media attention to the full-fledged "fishing wars" that were now raging in the Pacific Northwest.

In the fall of 1970, the battle over treaty rights would reach a dangerous climax. By this time, protesters had set up fishing camps at several sites along the rivers and streams of the Northwest. On the banks of the Puyallup River in Washington, a group of about 200 Indians and some white supporters had established one such camp from which they launched a series of fish-ins.

On several occasions, game wardens raided the site. To protect themselves, Indians organized an armed guard around the camp, an act that greatly provoked game wardens and local police officers. On September 9, some 100 law enforcement agents — wearing riot gear and wielding guns — descended on the camp. Shots rang out and a full-scale riot erupted. Officers beat the Indians with clubs and tossed tear gas into the crowd. One Indian protester threw a firebomb at a wooden bridge that spanned the river, sending it up in flames. Police arrested 55 adults and five youths and forced the rest of the protesters to abandon the site. Soon after the bloody encounter, officials bulldozed the fishing camp.

But the images of officials brutally attacking Indian protesters — images that had been beamed via television satellite into living rooms around the nation — weren't so easily erased. Among those shocked by what they saw were White House officials. The violent confrontation marked a crucial turning point in the fishing wars.

For decades, the tribes had urged the federal government to intervene in the conflict between state officials and Northwest peoples. Up to this point, U.S. officials had done little on Indians' behalf. But on September 18, 1970, nine days after the battle on the Puyallup River, the U.S. Justice Department filed a comprehensive lawsuit against the State of Washington for interfering with tribal fishing rights. Fourteen Northwest tribes were named as co-plaintiffs in the suit.

District Judge George Boldt, who was assigned the case, reportedly groused to a law clerk, "I don't want to hear any more of these damn Indian fishing cases." But he pursued the task with a thoroughness no one else had bothered with before: For months on end, he spent his nights and weekends reading Indian treaties and fishing rights cases dating back to the 19th century.

He learned something very interesting in the process. At the time of the 1854 treaties, fishing "in common with" meant "sharing equally" in the catch. In his landmark ruling of February 12, 1974 — known thereafter as the "Boldt decision" — the

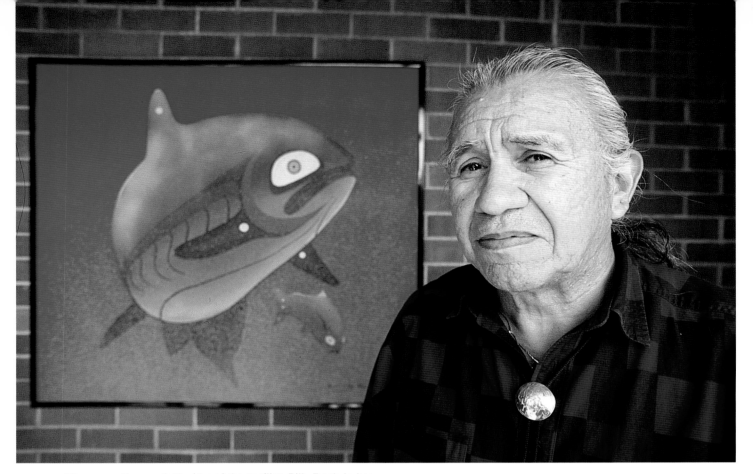

Like many others on both sides of the conflict, Billy Frank Jr. has put old animosities behind him.

judge declared that Indians were entitled to 50 percent of the fish that came to "usual and accustomed places." He ruled that the tribes could manage their own fisheries. He said that the state's earlier restrictions on Indian fishing were unlawful and refuted the idea that the Indian fishing threatened the resources for sportsmen.

Boldt's ruling was met with fury by those who opposed it. Anti-Indian forces such as the Ku Klux Klan, John Birch Society and sport-fishing associations assailed his decision. Some made it personal, burning Boldt's image in effigy and accusing him of having an Indian mistress. Non-Indian sport fishers harassed Indians, vandalizing their gear and ramming into their boats on the water. Still, the decision prevailed, and, in 1979, the Supreme Court affirmed Boldt's ruling.

It was a tremendous victory for Native peoples, not just in the Northwest but around the nation. Their success in defending their treaty rights brought a renewed sense of Native pride and hope that the Boldt decision would set an important precedent in similar cases. In fact, the Northwest tribes' triumph sparked a wave of Indian activism in other parts of the country, as Native peoples continued to demand recognition of long-ignored treaty rights.

But another chapter remained to be written in the history of the Northwest fishing wars, one that is still being written today. The court ruling had affirmed tribal fishing rights and established Indians as co-managers with state and federal agencies of this resource. The Native victory would mean nothing, however, if fish runs continued to decline. It was time to recognize that all of their fates — Native fishers, white fishers and the salmon themselves — were intertwined. Indians and whites needed to work together to protect the fish and their habitat.

Billy Frank Jr. still bears scars from some of the attacks he endured during the fishing wars. But like many others on both sides of the conflict, he has been able to put old animosities behind him. In 1974, Frank founded and became the first chairman of the Northwest Indian Fisheries Commission, a coalition of 19 tribal entities that works with government groups to restore salmon habitat.

"Rather than fighting, we're negotiating," says Frank, who now works cooperatively with the same fish and game agencies who sent him to jail more than 40 times. "Rather than suing each other, we're putting together teams and combining resources to properly manage the natural resources we all depend on."

As a symbol of both sides' commitment to a new partnership, Frank points to a traditional dugout canoe — *his* canoe — that is now on display at Wa He Lut Indian School at Frank's Landing, the site of so many "fish-ins" during the 1960s and '70s.

"In 1974, while I was working with the state and everybody, they always said, 'We're going to try to find your canoe,'" says Frank, who hadn't seen his boat since it was taken by state officials during a demonstration in 1964. "Then in 1980, on my birthday, they brought it back to me. They had found it in a warehouse in Seattle."

It had been 16 years. Even though the boat's wood had rotted to the point that it could no longer go on the river, Frank took it home.

"This boat tells a story," Frank says, "that there is recognition and understanding, a better understanding of the tribal side and of the state of Washington side. That they can understand better what the canoes mean to us. That we can sit at the table and start gaining a little trust with one another."

The veteran fishing rights activist remembers his father, Billy Frank Sr., once saying that if the salmon disappeared, there would be no more Indians. Billy Frank Jr. is not about to let that happen. He continues to devote his energies to preserving the fish runs and his people's cultural identity.

Moving from a situation of confrontation to cooperation hasn't happened overnight, Frank points out, and many challenges still lie ahead.

"It takes a lot of patience," Frank says, "but there's more good people than bad people, and the system will work if we all get in there and take part and stay committed. That's the only way we can get our salmon back and get our waters clean again." ◻

Rights *and* Wrongs

In 1924, American Indians were recognized as U.S. citizens and extended the same constitutional rights that all Americans now possess. But tribes also have a unique political relationship with the federal government that sets them apart from other cultural groups in the United States. That relationship is based in part on *sovereignty*, or tribal rights to self-government. It is also founded on the U.S. government's *trust responsibility* to tribes; that is, the tribes' trust that the federal government will fulfill certain promises it made to Native peoples in exchange for their lands.

This distinctive relationship has often brought Native Americans into conflict with non-Indians and state and local governments. For example, to non-Indian commercial fishers and to sports fishers in the Pacific Northwest, the struggle by Northwest Native peoples to exercise their treaty fishing rights — and thus avoid licensing requirements and other restrictions set by state authorities — seemed like an attempt to gain "special privileges." If we're a nation striving to provide equal rights for all, some argue, why grant Indians advantages that other groups are not permitted to enjoy?

But as Judge George Boldt pointed out in his landmark decision, ". . . the treaty fishing of plaintiff tribes is a reserved *right,* not a mere privilege." These and other rights were never granted by the United States; rather they were retained by Native peoples, original occupants of the continent, after ceding vast tracts of land to the United States through treaties.

AT ISSUE ★ ★ ★

Flawed as the treaty-making process was, the agreements still stand as legal documents made between equal nations and guaranteeing the rights of both parties. The U.S. Constitution recognizes treaties as the highest law in the land, alterable only by acts of Congress.

Some non-Indians maintain that the treaties are ancient history and, as such, they should be disregarded. But what can be said about a nation that doesn't honor its past commitments? If our government chooses to nullify rights assured to the first Americans, how secure can all citizens feel about the protections guaranteed us in another "ancient" document, the Bill of Rights?

As a nation, our destinies are tied up together. The invalidation of one group's rights threatens us all.

10

San Francisco, California ⚜ 1977

WHEELS OF JUSTICE

For decades, Americans with disabilities were unable to go to school with other children, get jobs like other adults or simply cross the street. Curbs, steps and stigmas stopped them everywhere they went. But on a spring day in 1977, some disabled residents of San Francisco decided they were tired of being barred from the rest of society. To make their point, they staged a dramatic month-long sit-in at a government building, demanding — and ultimately winning — civil rights for the nearly 50 million people with physical and mental handicaps living in the United States.

by LISA BENNETT

On April 5, 1977, Judy Heumann rolled her wheelchair through a crowd of 200 demonstrators who had gathered outside a government building in San Francisco. The protesters were demanding enforcement of a law that would guarantee Americans with disabilities access to public buildings. Heumann asked one person after another: "Did you bring your toothbrush?"

Jeff Moyer, a blind folk singer, said, "No. Why?"

"We're staying," said Heumann.

"It's news to me," said Moyer.

In fact, only a few people — like Mary Jane Owen, who walked with a white cane and wore a long black skirt and shawl that could double as a blanket — had been warned that there would be a sit-in at the department of Health, Education and Welfare (HEW) that day. Heumann hadn't wanted word to spread to HEW authorities or they might prevent the protesters from entering the building.

With or without their toothbrushes, demonstrators did enter the building to discuss their demands with HEW officials. And when security guards prepared to lock the doors at 6 o'clock that night, about 100 of them stayed right where they were, despite threats of arrest.

Many were in wheelchairs. Some were blind and some deaf. Others had mental disabilities or emotional ones. At home, a few had to rely on aides for everyday needs ranging from using the bathroom to turning over in bed.

Still, they were willing to stay the night or longer without beds, food or wheelchair-accessible bathrooms, for one simple reason: The law had the power to change their lives by literally opening doors that had long been closed to them.

At the time, few people with disabilities could count on that kind of access, as Judy Heumann, the sit-in's leader, could attest. Judy had been paralyzed from polio in childhood. When she was 5 years old, she was not allowed to attend an elementary school because the principal said her wheelchair would present a danger to other children in case of fire.

So she was schooled at home. A few hours a week, a teacher came to her; Judy spent the rest of her time reading and waiting for 3 o'clock when she could see her friends and attend Brownies.

She was, of course, lonely. But because this was the only life she knew, Judy did not think of herself as different from — or less able than — other children. Nor did her family and friends treat her as if

she were. But by 4th grade, when she was finally permitted to join her peers, she recognized that other people treated her differently because she sat in a wheelchair.

What other people could not so readily see, however, was that Judy was extremely intelligent. In fact, by age 10 she was reading at a high school level. Nonetheless, administrators at the new school Judy entered in 6th grade made plans to send her home. But this time, her mother organized with other parents and won the right for children with disabilities to stay in New York City public schools.

For Judy Heumann, it was the first of a lifetime of battles for access to the places and opportunities that most people take for granted. After high school, she fought for the right to attend college. And after college, she fought for the right to teach when school officials told her she wouldn't be able to manage a class.

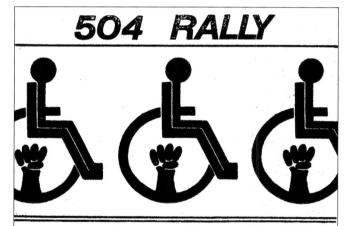

504 RALLY

NATIONWIDE DEMONSTRATION!!
NATIONWIDE DEMONSTRATION!!

Join us here in San Francisco:

TUESDAY, April 26
11:00 am to 1:00 pm
50 U.N. Plaza
Old Federal Building
Civic Center BART Station

With your support, we will win!

DISABLED RIGHTS

Protest leader Judy Heumann encouraged demonstrators to stay the course, however long it took to win.

"I'VE BEEN WORKIN' IN THE WORKSHOP"

The National Federation of the Blind (NFB) was founded in 1940 to promote the economic and social welfare of blind Americans. At the time, "the blind" were considered not just physically disabled, but mentally and emotionally impaired as well. Blind men and women were often denied entry to restaurants, theaters and hotels, as well as access to public transportation.

Job opportunities were also scarce, and many blind people labored in what were known as "sheltered workshops." Typically, workshop laborers were paid half the minimum wage to weave baskets, cane chairs and make mops. Social agencies running the workshops defended the low wages on the grounds that the work was therapeutic. But the NFB called the workshops exploitative and organized protests to demand better wages.

At the demonstrations, NFB members sang protest songs that mocked what they considered to be a paternalistic defense of the sheltered workshops. Following is one of the NFB's more popular songs, a spoof of "I've Been Workin' on the Railroad."

I've been workin' in the workshop, all the live-long day,
And with the wages that they pay me, it's just to pass
  my time away;
And when I ask about more money, they give me the
  big lie:
We'd like to give you lots of raises, but you'd lose your
  SSI.*

Work is therapy,
They keep telling me,
I've heard it till I've had my fill.

'Cause if it's therapy
I wish they'd let me be —
This therapy's a bitter pill.

*Social Security Insurance

Words by The (Pennsylvania) Liberty Alliance. Taken from *The National Federation of the Blind Song Book,* © 1991.

Although she triumphed in both these personal battles, Heumann remained deeply unsettled by the many obstacles that still blocked the paths of millions of capable people who happened to have a disability. And so, in the early 1970s, she began to fight on behalf of all Americans with disabilities.

The most important battle, which would culminate in the 1977 sit-in, was over access to federally funded buildings through enforcement of a piece of law referred to as "Section 504." In 1973, Congress had passed a routine spending bill authorizing funds for rehabilitation and training programs for the disabled. Within the bill was the "Section 504" provision, which prohibited discrimination against people with disabilities in programs that received federal funding.

"Section 504" was modeled on Title VI of the Civil Rights Act of 1964, which bars discrimination based on race, and Title IX of the Education Amendment of 1972, which forbids discrimination based on gender. But the provision had been inserted by legislative aides, rather than studied and debated by Congress. It appeared that many Congressional representatives had voted for the bill without realizing the monumental ramifications of the section.

When it came time to sign the regulations specifying how the law would be enforced, HEW officials realized that Section 504 would require significant changes — and costs. At public schools and federally-funded colleges, for example, wheelchair ramps would need to be added and restrooms modified so disabled people could attend classes. In essence, the law would prohibit a principal from telling someone like Judy Heumann that she could not attend school because she was in a wheelchair and, instead, require schools to become accessible. To avoid such a tremendous undertaking, the chief official at HEW simply avoided signing the regulations.

Disability activists like Heumann were not about to let a good law slip through their fingers. They formed the American Coalition of Citizens with Disabilities and began lobbying for enforcement. In 1975, they won their first apparent victory when presidential candidate Jimmy Carter promised that if elected, his HEW chief would sign the regulations. But when Carter was sworn into office in January 1977 and named Joseph Califano as HEW secretary, Califano balked. It had been four years since Congress had passed the original bill. Meeting in Washington, Judy Heumann and her colleagues decided they had had enough.

They agreed that they couldn't allow this to become an endless process. They had to set a specific deadline for the signing of the legislation. And they

Steps *to* Equality

FIRST PERSON

Among the more radical groups in the disability rights movement has been American Disabled for Attendant Programs Today (ADAPT). In 1990, ADAPT organized a series of demonstrations to press for passage of the Americans with Disabilities Act. During one rally in front of the U.S. Capitol, protesters threw themselves out of their wheelchairs and began crawling up the building's 83 marble steps. Each carried a scrolled paper with the opening words of the Declaration of Independence to present to lawmakers. It was a dramatic demonstration of the need for wheelchair access to public buildings.

Before the "crawl-up," ADAPT co-founder Michael Auberger addressed the 700 demonstrators from his motorized wheelchair at the bottom of the Capitol steps. Auberger recalled a 9th grade class trip that he had made to the Capitol before injuring his spinal chord in a bobsled accident.

Twenty years ago, I walked up these steps a wholly equal American citizen. Today I sit here with you as less than second-class citizens who are still legally discriminated against daily. The steps we sit before represent a long history of discrimination and indignities heaped upon disabled Americans. . . . Among us are those who have been forced to live in institutions against our will. There are those among us who have had our children taken away solely because we are disabled. We have been denied housing and jobs. These indignities and injustices must not go on. We will not permit these steps to continue to be a barrier to prevent us from the equality that is rightfully ours. The preamble to the Constitution does not say, "We the able-bodied people." It says, "We the people." We *are* the people.

(Above) Protestors leaving the HEW building were not allowed to return. Supporters kept a continuous presence outside the building to encourage those who remained inside. (Left) During a briefing on the fourth day of the sit-in, a woman (standing, left) uses sign language for the benefit of the deaf demonstrators in the group.

resolved to hold demonstrations around the country if the demand wasn't met.

With a deadline set for April 5, 1977, Heumann flew to California and began organizing with other activists who had experience in a range of social movements, including women's rights, union organizing and the fight for racial equality. They distributed flyers, planned speakers, made banners, informed the news media, arranged transportation, and warned transit workers to expect many riders with disabilities on the day of the demonstration.

Jeff Moyer, who had progressive vision loss, was one rider on the subway that morning. He carried a guitar, a bullhorn, a pencil and a scrap of paper, and, as he traveled, he scribbled the words to a song that had become an anthem for African Americans during the Civil Rights Movement. Rephrasing the lyrics for this cause, Moyer wrote:

> We won't stop till the battle is won
> And enforcement of the law begun
> Keep your eyes on the prize, hold on!
> Hold on, hold on —
> Keep your eyes on the prize, hold on!

At the rally, Moyer led the demonstrators in song, and the crowd listened to several speeches. Then Heumann urged everyone into the building that housed HEW's offices. Some hours later, officials threatened to have all of them charged with trespassing.

"Fine," Heumann replied, aware that, in these circumstances, their disabilities could be used to their advantage. "Just know that one among us is hemophiliac and could bleed to death if you hurt him."

Apparently unwilling to risk a public confrontation, police made no arrests. But still intent on gaining control, officials announced that food would not be allowed in; telephone lines would be cut off to outgoing calls; and protesters who left the building for any reason would not be allowed back in.

The news made some protesters nervous. But when journalists showed up to cover the event, Heumann, who had set up an office in an elevator shaft, reported confidently: "We're perfectly capable of staging a sit-in."

Similar messages were being conveyed at rallies in New York, Los Angeles, Seattle and Denver. Several hundred people also had staged a sit-in at the HEW headquarters in Washington, D.C. But on the second day, the D.C. protesters were forced out after being denied all food and drink except one doughnut and a cup of coffee.

But community support in San Francisco was swift and strong. Almost immediately, the Black Panthers delivered a pot of stew. McDonald's sent hamburgers. Safeway stores donated boxes of food. So did the staff of a lesbian cafe, the residents of a home for recovering drug addicts, and other groups. Two Catholic seminarians, dressed in blue robes, also showed up to prepare and serve meals. Soon the officials who had declared that no food would be permitted in were forced to open their doors to the outpouring of assistance.

The community continued to throw its support behind the protesters. A group of gay men who patrolled against gay-bashing incidents donated walkie-talkies. The state Department of Health sent 100 mattresses. A local congressman installed portable phones, designed for people in wheelchairs. And the mayor delivered portable showers, although the HEW director complained: "I'm not running a hotel here."

Religious leaders, city council members and the human rights commissioner held a vigil and press conference. The National Organization of Women, the National Association for the Advancement of Colored People, the Gray Panthers (a senior citizens organization), the Communist Party, the American Legion, labor unions and farm workers also voiced their support. And, outside, city residents held a flurry of rallies to show theirs.

(Above) Protestors waited on the streetside outside First Baptist Church, hoping to influence President Carter. *(Right)* The International Association of Machinists provided transportation around Washington, D.C.

With every day that passed, however, the demonstrators wondered whether they should stay on. Whether food would hold out. Whether the physical toll would be too high. Whether anyone was paying attention.

Judy Heumann was worried about reports that the HEW chief was considering weakening the regulations before signing them. She expressed this concern to two state Congressmen, George Miller and Phillip Burton, and they called an ad hoc congressional hearing on the subject, right at the site of the demonstration.

It was Friday, April 15, the 10th day of the sit-in. The national news media arrived. Several hundred supporters rallied outside. And an HEW representative outlined the changes the department was considering, including the possibility that people with

disabilities might be educated in "separate but equal" schools, instead of having existing schools adapted for them.

Heumann appeared at the witness table, fighting back tears.

"The lack of equity that has been provided to disabled individuals, and that now is even being discussed by the administration, is so intolerable that I can't quite put it into words," she began. "But I can tell you that every time you raise the issue of separate but equal, the outrage of disabled individuals across the country is going to continue, it is going to be united. There will be more takeovers of buildings until finally, maybe, you will begin to understand our position."

Four days later, as some 50 protesters stayed on in San Francisco, Heumann led a contingent of 20

others to Washington, D.C., in the hopes that they could take their case directly to Califano and Carter. Arriving at the airport, they were met by supporters from the International Machinists Union, who wheeled their chairs into the back of a rented Ryder truck. With nothing to hold onto but each other, their wheelchairs swerved across the floor as the driver wound his way through city traffic to Califano's house.

It was nearly midnight when they arrived. The driver opened the back door, and those on crutches and canes stepped down while those in wheelchairs were helped down via a hydraulic lift. Several neighbors turned on their lights. Then the protesters formed a circle and held candles in a silent vigil. A few minutes later, a police car arrived and asked the demonstrators to leave. But they refused and the police, seemingly uncertain of what to do, backed away and watched.

As the sun rose seven hours later, Heumann wheeled her chair to Califano's steps and called out: "Please open the door. I cannot get up your steps."

There was no reply. So she called out again. And again. Finally, an employee came to the door and said that Califano had left, apparently by the back door.

Exhausted and frustrated, but determined to fight on, the group returned to Califano's neighborhood another day and distributed flyers that charged him with blocking civil rights to people with disabilities. Again, they called to Califano from outside his door. But Califano refused to speak with them.

So they went to his office building. But federal guards saw them coming, locked the doors and stood in front of them, their legs spread wide apart to block their entry. Judy Heumann surveyed the scene in anger. At wit's end, she drove her chair into the door, backed up and rammed it again, while other protesters followed suit.

> The 25 days of protest helped bring years of effort to a successful close.

"These great big guards didn't know how to respond," recalled journalist Evan White. "They kicked their chairs to try to get them to stop."

The protesters moved to the next door. But guards blocked them there as well. They went on and tried the garage door. But, again, they were blocked.

They targeted President Jimmy Carter next. On a Sunday morning, they rolled and walked to the First Baptist Church, where President Carter worshiped, and waited for a chance to speak to him. Carter, however, entered through a side entrance and left using a rear one. His motorcade passed in front of the crowd, but the president did not look their way.

Several of the protesters cried in frustration and disappointment at being shunned. Still, they would not give up and called on White House staff members, HEW officials and members of Congress. The news media, meanwhile, increasingly reported on the issue. And finally the political pressure, which had been building for years, peaked.

On April 28, exactly 25 days after the demonstration began, a pay phone rang at the site of the San Francisco sit-in with the news: Califano had signed the regulations, unchanged, guaranteeing all Ameri-cans with disabilities access to schools, hospitals and other institutions that received federal funding.

"It was absolute delirium for us," recalls Raymon Uzeta. "Everyone's energy level went right through the roof. We were ecstatic, hugging and yelling. What a high."

Instead of going home, however, they stayed on two more days, waiting for the Washington contingent to return. Then, on April 30, they emerged from the building as one triumphant group while several hundred spectators applauded and cheered.

The physical toll the sit-in took on many was obvious. Mary Jane Owen, who had gone in blind but walking, came out in a wheelchair because she had tripped and injured her knee. Steven Handler-Klein, who had multiple sclerosis, was gravely ill after spending nearly a month deprived of care because he believed that his participation in this sit-in was the most important event of his life. But emotionally, most were stronger and happier than they'd ever been.

"Instead of seeing myself as a weak person," one demonstrator said, "I found my strength reinforced by others like me."

"I discovered something about myself that I didn't know," said another, " — that I count as a person."

As their leader, Judy Heumann regretted that she had remained in Washington to attend to business details and missed the victory march by those who staged what, to this day, remains the longest sit-in at a federal building in American history.

The rights that were won for people with disabilities that April were not the result of the San Francisco sit-in alone, she observed. As in most battles for civil rights, victory also required years of activism, coalition-building and the support of allies. But those 25 days helped bring years of effort to a successful and moving close.

In addition to the political and social benefits, the victory was deeply rewarding to the protesters on a very personal level. "It showed all of us how much we could do," reflected Heumann — no small success for a group of Americans long accustomed to being told by the larger society what they could not do. ▨

STORMING THE BARRICADES

AT ISSUE

While many groups have battled against legal barriers that have prevented their full participation, Americans with disabilities have struggled to remove physical barriers. Passage of Section 504 was a giant leap forward on the road to equal access to public facilities.

Since colonial days, Americans with mental and physical limitations typically have been pushed to the margins of society. Deemed uneducable, unemployable and socially unfit, thousands of disabled people were shut away in almshouses and later in state institutions. Such facilities were often places of neglect and abuse. They also promoted dependence.

But in the early 1800s, doctors and others working with blind and deaf individuals began to promote the idea that the disabled could be integrated into their communities and become self-sufficient. With these goals in mind, the first school for the blind opened its doors in Baltimore, Maryland, in 1812; five years later, a school for the deaf was established in Hartford, Connecticut. By the end of the century, disabled Americans began to form their own organizations, such as the National Association of the Deaf and the National Federation of the Blind. These coalitions were not charities; rather, they were self-led advocacy groups that promoted the interests of disabled citizens.

Disability rights protests during the early 20th century, however, were fragmented and sporadic. Disabled Americans engaged in civil disobedience for the first time in 1935, when the newly formed League for the Physically Handicapped organized sit-ins and picket lines to demand Works Progress Administration jobs. Following World War II, disabled veterans also organized and pressed for employment opportunities.

In the 1960s, the Independent Living Movement ushered in a new era of activism. The movement began at the University of California's Berkeley campus when a group of physically disabled students — many of them paraplegics and quadriplegics — joined forces and formed what they called "the Rolling Quads."

The students spent long hours strategizing about how to become more self-sufficient and less isolated from mainstream society. Their efforts eventually led to the formation of the Center for Independent Living (CIL) which helped anyone with disabilities become integrated into the larger community by providing housing assistance, transportation and other services. Run by people with disabilities, the CIL was based on the principle that "independence" meant everyone had the right to make their own decisions about how to live, no matter how serious their disabilities.

The Independent Living Movement gave birth to a new generation of disability rights activists. They demanded freedom from discrimination — a right granted women and racial, ethnic and religious minorities — and freedom from the segregation imposed by inaccessible buildings, transportation and sidewalks. Section 504 represented the coming together of these people with a new sense of what their rights were and what they could accomplish.

But Section 504 was just the beginning of changes to come. The crowning achievement of the growing disability rights movement was the passage in 1990 of the Americans with Disabilities Act (ADA), one of the most comprehensive pieces of civil rights legislation in history. Where Section 504 guaranteed people with disabilities access to schools, hospitals and other institutions that received federal funding, the ADA extended their access to employment, transportation and privately owned businesses, such as stores and restaurants.

Implementation of the ADA has been a long, difficult process that continues today. But its impact on the lives of millions of people has been significant, offering disabled Americans for the first time in our nation's history the promise of full citizenship under the law.

GOING TO BAT for GIRLS

Two hundred years ago, it was widely believed that women had a smaller capacity to learn than men. As a result, the educational system was geared primarily toward males. Over time, women fought against — and toppled — many of the barriers that prevented them from getting an equal education. But as recently as 30 years ago, they still faced some daunting hurdles. Studies showed that female students were being shortchanged from grade school through graduate school. In fact, many colleges and professional schools set limits on the number of young women they would admit. Others refused to admit women at all.

In 1972, Congress acted to eliminate gender discrimination in schools by passing what is referred to as Title IX of the Education Amendment Act. Title IX requires that federally funded schools give females the same opportunities as males in all education programs, including athletics. In principle, the law was simple. But getting schools to comply with Title IX has been another story. One family in Nebraska seeking equal resources for girls at their community high school found out just how resistant to change some people can be.

by **LISA BENNETT**

The events that changed Naomi Fritson's life — and the lives of high school students across Nebraska — began on a cold March night in 1992. Fritson, a part-time school bus driver, went to watch a girls' basketball game in the small farming town of Minden where she lives. But when she arrived at the school's main gym, Fritson was told that the game had been moved to a lesser facility known as the "girls' gym." The reason for the change: A boys' game had been rescheduled and the boys *always* played in the main gym.

The explanation unsettled her.

The main gym, after all, could seat about 500 spectators; the girls' gym only about 50. The main gym had a new sound system, a concession stand and a public restroom; the girls' gym had none of these features. Moreover, the main gym housed all

the locker rooms, which meant the girls had to change into their shirts and shorts and run outdoors — often in frigid temperatures — to the girls' gym.

These inequities troubled Fritson. Her own daughter, Sarah Casper, was about to begin high school. Fritson worried that the preferential treatment boys received at school would make Sarah feel she was somehow less important than her male peers or her two younger brothers.

Fritson raised the topic with other parents and learned that many of them had also noticed the difference in how young male and female athletes were treated at the high school. But no one, she found, was willing to speak up about it. Several mothers said simply: "It's only four years. You'll get used to it."

But Fritson wasn't about to "get used to" a situation that could harm her daughter. She was prepared

(Left) Naomi Fritson and Dean Casper made the commitment to provide equal sports opportunities for their daughter, Sarah Casper, whatever it took.

to fight for what was fair, even if it meant challenging authority and going against public opinion.

A community of about 2,700 people, Minden is dominated by cornfields as far as the eye can see. In late summer, the stalks tower head-high. In the evening, the dust from the fields rises up and meets the last rays of sun, creating dramatic red sunsets in the vast sky.

Minden is a community that takes great pride in its pioneer past. A sprawling museum in the center of town and billboards for miles around constantly remind residents that frontierspeople passed this way in the mid-1800s as they headed west in search of gold, religious freedom and adventure.

Naomi Fritson was born and raised here. In Fritson's family, her father made all the decisions, and her mother — like many women of her generation — quietly followed along. But Fritson had always had an irrepressible drive to think for herself. So, on a winter day in 1992, Fritson went home to the 1,000-acre corn and cattle farm where her family lives and fired off a letter to the school superintendent.

"Whether outright or subconsciously, these girls are going through the Minden system treated, and feeling, like second-class citizens," Fritson wrote. As evidence, she pointed out three examples of unequal treatment. First, the pep band routinely played at boys' games and rarely at girls' games. Second, girls

were required to play in the inferior gym. And, third, football games were scheduled for the most popular times — Friday and Saturday nights — while girls' volleyball games were held during the week when the crowds were smaller and the athletes would have to squeeze in homework after the game.

When Fritson met with the superintendent, he agreed that gender equity was important. But he argued that football had to be played on the weekend and girls' games during the week because fans were more interested in boys' sports than girls'.

The superintendent's response only fueled Fritson's anger. She pounded out another letter. People weren't naturally more interested in boys' sports than girls', she wrote. The school encouraged that attitude by treating female athletes as second-rate; they offered girls fewer teams to play on, inferior athletic equipment, poorly maintained fields, older buses, fewer and less experienced coaches, and less publicity.

It was true, the superintendent agreed, that girls were sometimes shortchanged when it came to resources. That was unfair and should be corrected. But one thing would not change, he insisted, and that was Friday night football. The school depended on income from its fans, and they were most likely to attend weekend games.

Fritson attended more meetings and wrote more letters, but still nothing happened. Then she remembered a poster she had seen hanging in a school hallway. It said if students felt they had been discriminated against, they could file a Title IX complaint with the Office of Civil Rights.

Fritson had never heard of Title IX, but she soon learned it was a federal law that required all public schools to offer equal opportunities to boys and girls or lose funding. Many Title IX battles focused on the funding of girls' sports programs. Since its introduction in 1972, Title IX had been quietly opening doors for female athletes, and they were bounding through.

In fact, when Fritson attended high school in the 1960s, there were no girls' athletic teams in Minden at all. Administrators had decided years before that sports made girls "unladylike." Minden had indeed come a long way since Fritson's school days. But as far as she was concerned, it still had a long way to go in creating a level playing field for girls.

However, Fritson didn't want to file a formal complaint. Her kids attended the schools, and she loved

Liberty to Learn

Because women had small brains, advanced education would only be wasted on them. Such was the reasoning of early American society. Furthermore, conventional wisdom held, women risked ruining their figures, their complexions and — worst of all — their reproductive capacities by engaging in rigorous mental exercise.

During the 19th century, women increasingly challenged these notions and fought for the right to attend institutions of higher learning. Among the male allies lending support to their cause was writer and editor George W. Curtis. During the 25th anniversary celebration in 1890 of the founding of Vassar College — one of the first women's colleges in the United States — Curtis challenged the belief that higher education would cause women to abandon their "natural sphere" of domestic duties.

FIRST PERSON

We may be very sure that we shall never know the sphere of any responsible human being until he has perfect freedom of choice and liberty of growth. All we can clearly see is that the intellectual capacity of women is an inexplicable waste of reserved power, if its utmost education is justly to be deprecated as useless or undesirable. . . .

And if any skeptic should ask, "But can delicate woman endure the hardship of a college course of study?" it is a woman who ingeniously turns the flank of the questioner with a covert sarcasm at her own sex — "I would like you to take thirteen hundred young men, and lace them up, and hang ten to twenty pounds of clothes upon their waists, perch them on three-inch heels, cover their heads with ripples, chignons, rats, and mice, and stick ten thousand hairpins into their scalps. If they can stand all this they will stand a little Latin and Greek."

her job working as a bus driver. She suggested that the administration ask a Title IX representative to discuss the issue with them. The school superintendent agreed, and at the end of the meeting, Fritson left with a copy of the law in her hands.

That night, she and her husband sat at the kitchen table and looked the law over. It said that boys and girls should have equal opportunities in the exercise of their athletic interests, the use of equipment, travel arrangements, coaching opportunities, locker room and competitive facilities, publicity and scheduling of games.

On almost every point she had raised, Fritson realized there was a federal law backing her up. Now that administrators were better informed about the law as well, she was optimistic that things would change. But months went by and still nothing happened. Fritson filed a complaint.

The Office of Civil Rights had assured her that the complaint would be confidential. But soon her name showed up in the newspaper. When Fritson contacted the Office of Civil Rights to ask what

(Left) The first women's college basketball teams were organized in 1893. Despite many obstacles, including charges of being "unladylike," the sport had become a staple of high school programs by the mid-20th century. (Right) Naomi worried that the school's preferential treatment of boys' athletics would make Sarah feel less important than her younger brothers, Andrew and Seth.

happened, she recalls, they said her name had slipped out. In a large city, it might have been a minor problem. In this small town, it was a big one.

People in Minden, surrounding communities and across the state erupted in fury — not at the school's alleged discrimination against girls but at Fritson. As one television reporter put it, she had challenged "a nearly sacred ritual" — Friday night football — and had "the gall" to ask: Why can't boys and girls share the weekend spot? Meanwhile, rumors spread that her demands for equality could lead to cuts in football, a sport one local minister is said to have described as "Nebraska's state God."

Newspapers published demeaning cartoons, caricaturing Fritson as a crank, and people posted them in stores. Unknown voices woke her with obscene calls in the middle of the night. When she attended sports events, other parents avoided sitting near her. Boys shouted obscenities at her as she walked across the school grounds. Even her father told people he was ashamed of her, adding: "I don't know how I failed in bringing her up."

Fritson wasn't the only family member who felt the sting of the attacks. Sarah didn't talk much about her feelings, but her mother knew the controversy was hard on her. Since Fritson had begun this battle, Sarah had grown increasingly isolated.

"I thought I had all these friends," Sarah later told a newspaper reporter, "and all of a sudden, they wouldn't look at me."

Worried that she was ruining her daughter's high school years, Fritson broke down in tears. Yet she couldn't imagine sitting quietly by while the school system treated Sarah and other girls unfairly. For a mother, it was an impossible dilemma: She could fight for her daughter's rights and subject her to the community's wrath or give up the battle and let her daughter submit to gender discrimination. Either way, Sarah would suffer.

Sarah secretly wished her mother would postpone her fight until she was out of high school. Then, one day, something happened to change her mind. Sarah had worn a T-shirt to gym class that read "Title IX Now." Some classmates, who equated Title IX with an attack on football, stole the T-shirt from her locker. When Sarah learned that it was a former close friend of hers who had arranged the scheme, she was shocked and hurt.

Sarah came home in tears. That's it, Fritson decided. It's over. But the T-shirt incident had stoked Sarah's own determination to change the system. She asked her mother to keep fighting.

Title IX helped pave the way for the growing field of women's sports. *(Left)* Fullback Luisana Cruz was one of four female varsity football players during the 1999 season at Lincoln High in Los Angeles. *(Above)* The U.S. team defeated China in the final game of the 1999 Women's World Cup soccer tournament. *(Above right)* Tara Mounsey, captain of Concord High School's undefeated, state-championship hockey team, was the 1995–96 New Hampshire Player of the Year.

Soon after, Fritson and Sarah discovered they were not alone in their battle. In Omaha, Nebraska's largest city, two men also had been fighting for female athletes by supporting girls' softball.

Ron Osborn was a successful men's softball player who had begun coaching women's softball at local universities to earn extra money and gain access to a gym. He repeatedly heard parents ask: Why isn't softball offered in high schools, where the girls might have a chance to win a scholarship? To his mind, the young women of Nebraska were being prevented from fulfilling their athletic potential. And he wasn't going to sit back and watch that happen to his daughter.

So Osborn and Sherm Posca, a child psychiatrist, put together a plan: With the help of supporters, they would raise money, buy uniforms for players, and encourage parents to run their own teams to show schools that girls were interested in softball. Then they would ask the schools to sponsor the teams.

Almost immediately, 40 private teams sprang up, including one that came together around Naomi Fritson's kitchen table. She and Sarah brainstormed a list of possible players and invited them to try out.

Fritson and her husband, Dean Casper, plunked down several thousand dollars for bats, balls and mitts. Dean also coached the team, while Fritson shuttled the girls to and from games. Sarah did her part by joining the newly formed team.

Their decision demanded sacrifices. Sometimes, Dean stood behind home plate watching other farmers drive by with their harvested crops and felt he should be home working, too. But he believed that Sarah and other girls should have the same opportunities boys did. The work would have to wait.

All told, 13 Minden girls joined the team. Under the shadow of a giant grain silo looming over center field, the girls cracked balls, pulled down high-flies and learned how to pitch. They ended their first season with a winning record.

Believing they had proven girls' interest in softball, Dean and Naomi asked the school to sponsor the team. They pointed out that this would balance the number of sports teams available to boys and girls, which then stood at four to three. But the

MEDICAL BREAKTHROUGH

Elizabeth Blackwell, the first woman to receive a degree from a medical college, helped pave the way for women seeking the same educational — and professional — opportunities as men. Blackwell was rejected from 29 schools of medicine because of her sex. Finally, a small medical college in Geneva, New York, agreed to accept her as a student in the fall of 1847. Blackwell wrote an account of the long and frustrating admissions process, including advice she received about how to circumvent the seemingly insurmountable hurdle of being born a female.

During these fruitless efforts my kindly Quaker adviser, whose private lectures I attended, said to me: "Elizabeth, it is of no use trying. Thee cannot gain admission to these schools. Thee must go to Paris and don masculine attire to gain the necessary knowledge." Curiously enough, this suggestion of disguise made by good Dr. Warrington was also given me by Doctor Pankhurst, the Professor of Surgery in the largest college in Philadelphia. He thoroughly approved of a woman's gaining complete medical knowledge; told me that although my public entrance into the classes was out of the question, yet if I would assume masculine attire and enter the college he could entirely rely on two or three of his students to whom he should communicate my disguise, who would watch the class and give me timely notice to withdraw should my disguise be suspected.

But neither the advice to go to Paris nor the suggestion of disguise tempted me for a moment. It was to my mind a moral crusade on which I had entered, a course of justice and common sense, and it must be pursued in the light of day, and with public sanction, in order to accomplish its end.

FIRST PERSON

The Minden Whippets girls' track team were the 1996 Nebraska State Champions.

board rejected the appeal, saying there were too few area teams for Minden girls to play.

Fritson was nearly at her wits' end. Her campaign had dragged on for three years. The complaint she had filed with the Office of Civil Rights had not produced the changes she wanted, and Sarah was about to enter her senior year. The only thing left to do was file a lawsuit.

The Fritson-Caspers had talked with lawyers before, but no one offered much encouragement. Then Fritson met Kristen Galles. Formerly a softball player for Creighton University in Omaha and now a lawyer, Kristen knew the thrill of being a female athlete. She was also well acquainted with the Title IX law, and she was confident that Naomi and Sarah could win this case.

So, in April 1995, the Fritson-Caspers and Galles made history, filing one of the first Title IX law-suits against any high school in the country. Supporting them in the case was the National Women's Law Center in Washington, D.C.

The community was outraged. The superintendent denounced the lawsuit's charges. Parents wrote to the local papers, saying that "the girls just want to be left alone." And one Minden resident wrote Fritson, "You've had your day in the sun. Now find a rock and crawl under it."

But no matter what people said, Fritson knew the law was on her side. And justice, she believed, was just a matter of time. A flurry of lawsuits were being filed around the country on behalf of girls in high school and college athletic programs.

About a year later, recognizing a growing movement toward equity in school sports, the Minden school district administrators offered a settlement. They promised to start a girls' softball team, offer equal equipment to girls, provide comparable transportation to and scheduling of games, hire equally experienced coaches, give the same amount of publicity to girls' and boys' teams, and pay Fritson $75,000 for attorney fees and damages.

"Minden felt that it was in the best interests of all concerned that this matter be settled in order to move the school district forward," Minden school superintendent Scott Maline told the press.

Fritson was relieved that her long, difficult struggle was over. She still smiles when she remembers attending the first Minden High School girls' softball game. "They lost, but they didn't care," she recalls. "They played their hearts out."

The family's legal victory didn't end in Minden. Their lawsuit, along with three more their lawyer filed against other Nebraska schools, put administrators throughout the state on notice. Fearing similar legal challenges, several dozen Nebraska schools took it upon themselves to improve their girls' sports programs and add softball.

> Fritson still smiles when she remembers the first Minden High girls' softball game.

As it turned out, Sarah Casper never had the opportunity to reap the rewards of their victory; she had graduated by the time Minden High School made any changes. But she is satisfied knowing that other young female athletes are benefiting from them now. She says the experience taught her a lot about what happens when you buck the system.

"I learned how standing up for something you believe in can cause lots of problems, and how things can get a whole lot worse before they get better," Sarah told a newspaper reporter. "You see just how much people hate change."

As for Naomi Fritson, she looked through her photo albums after this battle ended and realized that four years were missing. Since then, she has dedicated herself to catching up on family life. But she never doubts that she did the right thing.

"Everybody wonders what their function in life is," she says. "For me, I think this was it." ⊠

EQUALITY NOW

Formed in 1966, the National Organization of Women (NOW) sought "to take the actions needed to bring women into the mainstream of American society now ... in fully equal partnership with men." Providing girls with the same educational opportunities as boys was one of the goals outlined in NOW's founding statement of purpose.

WE BELIEVE that it is as essential for every girl to be educated to her full potential of human ability as it is for every boy — with the knowledge that such education is the key to effective participation in today's economy and that, for a girl as for [a] boy, education can only be serious where there is expectation that it will be used in society. We believe that American educators are capable of devising means of imparting such expectations to girl students. Moreover, we consider the decline in the proportion of women receiving higher and professional education to be evidence of discrimination. This discrimination may take the form of quotas against the admission of women to colleges and professional schools; lack of encouragement by parents, counselors and educators; denial of loans or fellowships; or the traditional or arbitrary procedures in graduate and professional training geared in terms of men, which inadvertently discriminate against women. We believe that the same serious attention must be given to high school dropouts who are girls as to boys.

REE GOD'S WIF

THE BATTLE OF SPANISH FORK

Federal law prohibits employment discrimination founded on race, religion, gender, national identity, disability and age. No such federal legal protection exists, however, on the basis of sexual orientation, and gay men and lesbians have been denied and fired from jobs because of this aspect of their identities. In recent decades, they have increasingly challenged discrimination and asserted their right to equal protection under the law. One teacher who decided to fight a local school district that threatened her job and freedom of expression because she was lesbian found herself in the middle of a controversy that would divide her entire community.

by LISA BENNETT

Wendy Weaver (front left) led the Spanish Fork High School volleyball team to the Utah State Championship in 1988.

On Saturday, May 31, 1997, Wendy Weaver, the most successful coach in the history of Spanish Fork High School, telephoned her volleyball team to remind them that summer training camp would begin the following Monday.

"Can I ask you a question?" one player said.

"Sure," Weaver said.

"Are you gay?"

Weaver paused. In her 17 years as a teacher and coach at Spanish Fork, no one had ever asked that question and she was unsure of how to answer it. If she said it was none of the student's business, it would suggest there was something shameful about being gay. If she said, no, it would be a lie. So she told the truth.

"Yes, I am."

"Then I can't play on your team," replied the student, who was about to be a senior.

"Why not?" Weaver asked.

"I don't want to be around it," the student said.

"Around what?" asked Weaver. "Nothing will be different than it was before."

"I just can't do it," the student said definitively.

Disappointed, Weaver hung up the phone at her home in Salem, Utah, where a neighbor's horse grazed several yards away, and the towering white tips of the Rocky Mountains looked almost within reach. For most of her life, Weaver had behaved exactly the way "good people" were expected to. As the youngest of 10 children raised on a dairy farm in southern Idaho, she willingly helped with farm chores. As a high school student, she became a cheerleader, junior class president and president of the National Honor Society.

She attended a religious college, Brigham Young University, in Provo, Utah, and became a devout Mormon, or member of the Church of Jesus Christ of Latter Day Saints, where she both attended services and taught Sunday school.

She became a teacher at 21; she married at 23; and six weeks later, she and her husband took in the first of 30 foster children before bearing a son and adopting a daughter of their own. In 1995, a school administrator nominated the couple for a "Family of the Year" award. Meanwhile, Weaver led the Spanish Fork volleyball team to four state championships.

For many of those years, however, Weaver also quietly struggled with the feeling that she was a lesbian. She tried to fight it, knowing that her religion and most people in the largely Mormon community of Spanish Fork condemned gay and lesbian relationships. But as time went on, it became more difficult. Finally, she and her husband divorced, and she moved in with a female partner, Rachel Smith.

In Weaver's mind, this decision did not stop making her a good person. In fact, she believed it made her a better person because she was living more

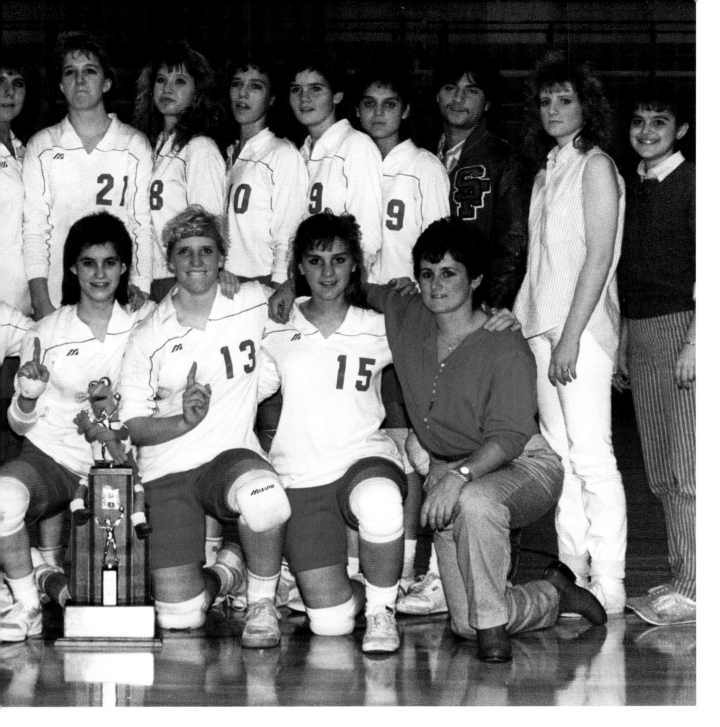

honestly than she had before. Still, she did anticipate some negative reactions to her and Smith's relationship. Her player's decision to quit the team was the first obvious one — and unbeknownst to her, a sign of more serious trouble ahead.

On July 21, the school principal, Robert Wadley, called Weaver into his office and announced that he would no longer permit Weaver to coach. His decision, he said, was in the best interest of the school, the students and the district.

Recognizing that this made little sense based on her record, Weaver asked if he had received any complaints about her coaching.

"No," Wadley said.

"Then why?" she asked again.

"My perception of you has changed," said Wadley, refusing to discuss the matter further.

Weaver left his office saddened and stunned. The next day, she would face more bad news. In a meeting at the school district headquarters, Almon Mosher, the director of human resources, read her a

Spanish Fork High School

July 21, 1997

Wendy Weaver
759 S. 410 E.
Salem, Utah 84653

Dear Wendy:

This is a follow-up memo to confirm our conversation on this date, wherein I informed you that I will not be assigning you to coach volleyball this year.

After a great deal of thought, I have determined that it will be in the best interest of the students, the school and the district if I assign someone else to that task.

I appreciate the time and energy that you have put into coaching in the past. I wish you the best as you make the transition to other pursuits.

Sincerely,

Bob Wadley
Bob Wadley
Principal

letter that instructed her not to talk about her sexual orientation or "anything concerning that subject" with students, teachers or parents. If she did, he continued, she could be fired for it.

Mosher gave her a copy of the letter and said another copy would be placed in her file. Weaver left the meeting in disbelief that she could lose her coaching job and the right to talk about her personal life in the course of two days, simply because she chose to live her life with another woman.

As she talked the incident over at home, she also grew worried that she could easily violate the gag order. For example, she thought, if she went out with Smith — to a ball game, the supermarket or a dinner party — and another parent perceived them to be a couple, that could be construed as a public statement about her sexual orientation and put her job in jeopardy.

Although Weaver knew little about the experiences of other gay and lesbian teachers at the time, many of them, she would discover, faced largely the same predicament that she did. In short, they were forced to hide their sexual orientation or run the risk of being fired or forced out of their jobs because of it.

In some cases, such fierce opposition to gay and lesbian teachers stemmed from religious beliefs that homosexuality is immoral. In others, it stemmed from prejudice, or unsubstantiated generalizations, such as the idea that the presence of a gay or lesbian teacher could alter a student's sexual orientation. And in some, it was fueled by both religion and prejudice.

A growing number of teachers had begun to challenge this opposition by coming out, or openly identifying themselves as gay or lesbian, at the time that Weaver responded to her student's question honestly. But the risks of doing so were, and still are, extremely high because there is no federal law that prohibits employment discrimination against gay and lesbian people. Although some states do have such laws, Utah is not one of them, so Weaver had no simple legal recourse. She was, by and large, in the same position as the majority of gay and lesbian teachers, with one significant exception: Unlike most who were forced out or pressured into silence by word of mouth, she had a letter that documented the school's position against her.

When Doug Worthham, director of Utah's Gay, Lesbian, Straight Education Network (GLSEN), heard about Weaver's situation, he tracked her down and introduced her to Carol Gnade, the executive director of Utah's American Civil Liberties Union (ACLU). Weaver and her partner met with Gnade in Salt Lake City. Gnade told them that she thought the letter gave Weaver the evidence she needed to win a lawsuit against the school for violation of her constitutional right of freedom of expression. Moreover, she said, the ACLU would be willing to fight Weaver's case on behalf of gay and lesbian teachers nationwide.

However, Gnade warned, Weaver had best think hard about whether she was prepared for a legal battle that was bound to set off a storm of controversy — especially in the conservative community of Spanish Fork.

With that question in mind, Weaver and Smith returned to their Salem home, where a four-foot-high frame displaying photos of their children greets everyone who walks in the front door. Between them, Weaver and Smith have six boys and one girl. The couple worried what would happen to their children if Weaver filed a suit against the school. Would they be harassed or embarrassed by the media attention and community gossip?

On the other hand, what would happen if she did not file suit and sought, instead, to protect her job by keeping her private life hidden? By accepting the gag order, Weaver felt that she would have to act as

Weaver said simply: "All I want is to have the freedom to live my private life as I choose."

JOB ORIENTATION

In 1981, Wisconsin became the first state to adopt a law protecting gay men and lesbians from discrimination. By the year 2000, ten more states had passed similar laws.

SECTION 17: It is discrimination because of sexual orientation:
1. For any employer, labor organization, licensing agency or employment agency or other person to refuse to hire, employ, admit or license, or to bar or terminate from employment, membership or licensure any individual, or to discriminate against an individual in promotion, compensation or in terms, conditions or privileges of employment because of the individual's sexual orientation.

To Serve with Honor

NEVER AGAIN
6 JULY 1943

NEVER FORGET
22 JUNE 1988

A GAY VIETNAM VETERAN

WHEN I WAS IN THE MILITARY
THEY GAVE ME A MEDAL FOR KILLING TWO MEN
AND A DISCHARGE FOR LOVING ONE.

On March 6, 1975, Leonard Matlovich, a United States Air Force sergeant awarded the Purple Heart for service in Vietnam, handed his captain a letter that began:

"After some years of uncertainty, I have arrived at the conclusion that my sexual preferences are homosexual as opposed to heterosexual. I have also concluded that my sexual preferences will in no way interfere with my Air Force duties."

Captain Dennis Collins slumped in his chair and said, "What does this mean?"

"This means *Brown* v. *Board of Education*," said Matlovich, referring to the landmark 1954 U.S. Supreme Court case that declared it unconstitutional for public schools to reject or segregate students on the basis of race.

Matlovich argued it was also unconstitutional for the U.S. military to reject service personnel on the basis of their sexual orientation — something they had done since World World II by issuing a dishonorable discharge to anyone thought to be gay or lesbian. His letter, which asserted that his sexual orientation was irrelevant to

his extraordinary record of service, was a direct challenge to that policy.

Six months later, Matlovich appeared on the cover of *Time* magazine, dressed in uniform, his medals clearly in view. The photograph was accompanied by four simple words: "I am a homosexual."

Two months later, he was discharged. He filed an appeal with a federal district court judge. But the judge upheld his dismissal. Matlovich continued to appeal the case until, three years later, it reached the U.S. Court of Appeals, which ruled that his dismissal was illegal and ordered the federal district judge to reconsider the case. The judge took two years to issue his order: The Air Force had to reinstate him.

The Air Force vowed to fight the order all the way to the Supreme Court. Expecting to win but hoping to avoid the cost, they offered Matlovich a cash settlement of $160,000. Sorely in need of money five years after his dismissal, and fully aware of his poor odds at the nation's highest court, Matlovich accepted, ending this particular battle but not the war.

Inspired by Matlovich's pioneering action, numerous gay and lesbian service members continued to challenge the military's ban against them, but with limited success. During the 1980s the military dismissed 17,000 gay and lesbian service members. Meanwhile, two internal Pentagon reports found that gays and lesbians posed no security risk, as had previously been alleged, and the public debate about the ban against gays in the military intensified.

In 1992, Col. Margarethe Cammermeyer was discharged after 26 years of exemplary service in the armed forces when she disclosed that she was a lesbian. Cammermeyer won a significant victory on behalf of gay and lesbian serv-

ice person-
nel when,
in 1994, a
federal district
judge ruled that the
military policy that had led to her dismissal
was based on prejudice and unconstitutional. Other gay men and lesbians were winning similar lawsuits.

A year prior to the Cammermeyer judi-
cial decision, the military replaced its ban
on gays with a new policy. Entitled "Don't
Ask, Don't Tell, Don't Pursue," this policy
declared that gays and lesbians could
serve as long as they did not say or do
anything to identify themselves as such.

But rather than improving life for gay
and lesbian service personnel, the new
policy made it worse. Discharges increased 92 percent in the first five years
after the "Don't Ask, Don't Tell" policy
was invoked, according to the Service-
members Legal Defense Network, which
monitors the military's treatment of gays
and lesbians. Harassment, including
death threats, verbal gay-bashing and
physical assault, has also increased. In
1999, a fellow enlisted man beat Private
Barry Winchell to death with a baseball
bat while he was sleeping because
Winchell was gay.

The long battle by gay men and lesbians to serve their country without being
forced to conceal a part of their identity
continues today as they challenge the
government's "Don't Ask, Don't Tell" policy in the courts. Leonard Matlovich, who
spurred on the struggle more than 25
years ago, died in 1988. But his words
supporting the cause endure. His tombstone reads: "When I was in the military,
they gave me a medal for killing two men,
and a discharge for loving one."

if she were ashamed of herself, which she was not.
Moreover, she would teach her children that they,
too, should be ashamed of their family, which was
an idea she could not bear. So the answer was clear:
She had to fight.

About six weeks later, the ACLU filed a lawsuit on
Weaver's behalf against the Nebo School District,
charging administrators with violation of her constitutional rights to freedom of expression, by asserting
that she could not discuss her sexual orientation
even off school grounds; to privacy, by interfering
with her personal life; and to equal protection under
the law, by imposing a condition on her employment
that was not also imposed on other teachers.

It is always news when a teacher files a lawsuit
against a school; it is very big news when a lesbian
teacher files a lawsuit against a school in a state pop-
ularly known as "Mormon country." Indeed,
Mormonism seems to impact all walks of life in
Utah, including the schools, where many school
administrators play active roles as bishops in their
local churches and many students receive religious
instruction on or near school grounds. And on the
question of sexuality, Mormon teaching is very
clear: Same-gender relations are against God's law.

In late October, the ACLU organized a news conference in Salt Lake City, the state capital, and invited Weaver to appear. At the press conference, she
faced a row of television cameras and newspaper
reporters who would broadcast news of the lawsuit
nationwide. When asked what had prompted her to
file the suit, Weaver said simply: "All I want is to
have the freedom to live my private life as I choose."

When it was time to return to the classroom a
few days later, Weaver was nervous but also
had a sense of conviction that she had done
the right thing. She took a walk through the building to try to defuse the tension and face any awk-
ward moments that were bound to arise as she
encountered faculty and students for the first time
after the news broadcast.

A few teachers gave her silent hugs of support as
she walked through the hallways. The principal suggested that they try not to have any hard feelings
while they waited for the courts to settle the conflict. And one student, whom she knew well, asked
as he passed Weaver outside the lunchroom:

"Do you have a girlfriend, Ms. Weaver?"

"Yes," she said.

"Me, too," he replied.

At home that day, Weaver was pleased to find a few letters had arrived in the mail, praising her courage to do what she believed was right. But these early gestures of support were soon followed by some crushing news: A group of about 100 parents and grandparents had started a petition protesting the school's employment of Weaver, any openly gay or lesbian teacher, or any other individual whose perceived morality they deemed to be objectionable. The group had even hired a lawyer to represent them.

"We have a say in what our kids are taught, in class or by example," said Roxanne Barney, a parent who withdrew her child from Weaver's psychology class as soon as word of her sexual orientation spread. Barney was now urging others to do the same.

In the weeks to follow, the group's petition circulated throughout the school and community; dozens of editorials and letters to the editor were published in the local newspapers; and, at homes and work, residents discussed the controversy.

> The petition stated, in part: "We believe that diversity and individuality are qualities that ... enable us to realize our full humanity."

Parents who knew Weaver well came to her defense. "Those of us parents who had children in the volleyball program almost unanimously said, 'What's sexual orientation got to do with her ability to coach volleyball?'" recalls Brent Kidman, who had two daughters on Weaver's team. "I can't say that we all agreed with her lifestyle, or understood it, but we certainly weren't afraid of her because of the good experiences our kids had with her in the past."

The majority of parents in Spanish Fork, however, did not have children in the volleyball program, and many of them signed the petition against her. Meanwhile Laurie Wood, an English professor at Utah Valley State College, started a counter-petition in support of Weaver, which stated, in part: "We believe that diversity and individuality are qualities that enrich our lives and enable us to realize our full humanity. We also believe that a community that alienates and ostracizes individuals does not reflect charitable and ethical values as we understand them." Both sides also promised to turn out for a public debate at the next school board meeting.

FIRST PERSON | UNITED WE STAND

In 1997, the National Gay and Lesbian Task Force presented Coretta Scott King with an award for her commitment to civil rights. In accepting the award, King recalled her late husband's message of universal fellowship.

My husband understood that all forms of discrimination and persecution were unjust and unacceptable for a great democracy. He believed that none of us could be free until all of us were free, that a person of conscience had no alternative but to defend the human rights of all people. I want to reaffirm my determination to secure the fullest protection of the law for all working people, regardless of their sexual orientation. . . . [I]t is right, just, and good for America.

Many of these courageous [gay and lesbian] men and women were fighting for my freedom at a time when they could find few voices for their own, and I will always remember and honor their contributions. . . .

I still hear from people who claim to be followers of Martin Luther King, Jr., but who think I should be silent about the human rights concerns of gays and lesbians. All I can do is tell these folks that the civil rights movement that I believe in thrives on unity and inclusion, not division and exclusion. All of us who oppose discrimination and support equal rights should stand together to resist every attempt to restrict civil rights in this country.

Students met at the Kidmans' house to coordinate their support for Coach Weaver.

few hours before the meeting, several television vans with five-story-high antennas pulled up outside the district office, preparing to broadcast their coverage statewide. An estimated 200 parents and other residents filed into the district office. Weaver stayed home on the advice of her lawyers, who were concerned about her safety.

Matthew Hilton, the lawyer representing the parents' group opposed to Weaver, delivered the petition against her to the board, reporting that it had been signed by 2,678 residents.

"It makes no sense to us to spend years creating one type of moral climate in our home [only] to have it directly or indirectly destroyed in our schools," he argued, and applause broke out.

Then Larraine Sands, another parent, stood up and countered Hilton's argument by saying: "The moral issue I'm concerned about here is the example we're setting for our own children regarding respect and tolerance for those whose beliefs are different from ours."

Again, applause broke out, revealing a community divided between those who believed that being gay or lesbian was wrong, and those who believed that being intolerant of gay and lesbian people was wrong. The school board, obliged to wait for the outcome of the lawsuit, listened without comment.

After the meeting, the controversy intensified again as rumors and allegations spread that Weaver had done numerous improper things with her play-

ers, such as discouraging them from dating boys and encouraging them to have lesbian relationships. These accusations angered many of the young women on Weaver's team, who knew the rumors to be false. They organized a press conference to denounce the allegations and praise their coach as a positive role model.

Weaver was buoyed by the support from her players. Yet she was also saddened by the public attacks that focused on such a narrow part of her identity.

"What bothers me," she said, "is I'm not Wendy Weaver anymore. I'm 'the lesbian teacher.' It's not who I am. I'm a teacher, a mother, and I was a coach.... The gay issue has become a focal point, but it shouldn't be. I wish I would be judged ... by my performance on the job like anyone else would be."

One consolation during this stressful period was that Weaver and Smith's children seemed to be weathering the controversy extremely well. While the parents of a couple of their children's friends forbade them to set foot in the Weaver-Smith house, the majority of their neighbors and church community were very supportive.

Weaver and Smith did their best to be open with their children about everything that was happening. However, at the time, their children were still quite

Following their victory, the Weaver-Smith family rode in Salt Lake City's Gay Pride Day parade.

young and didn't understand the full implications of the lawsuit.

"They mostly thought it was pretty cool that their moms were on TV and getting all this attention," Smith later recalled. But otherwise, they were absorbed in pursuing their own interests — riding their bikes and having water fights. Smith herself, however, was not unscathed by the controversy.

A highly rated collegiate sports official, Smith suddenly found herself dropped from several basketball conferences, without explanation. She felt that her removal from the officiating schedules was a direct result of the suit. Smith was also dealing with other personal difficulties as her parents adjusted to her announcement that she was lesbian and the very public spotlight that had now been shone on the whole family.

As the public opinion debate raged on, it finally came time for a ruling in Weaver's case. On November 5, 1998, U.S. District Senior Judge Bruce S. Jenkins handed down his verdict, saying: "The 'negative reaction' some members of the community may have to homosexuals is not a proper basis for discriminating against them. . . . Although the Constitution cannot control prejudices, neither this court nor any other court should directly or indirectly legitimize them." Furthermore, Jenkins said, the district had violated Weaver's right to free expression and equal protection under the law. He then ordered the school to withdraw the gag order and offer Weaver her coaching position again.

When Weaver's lawyer called with the news, she was elated — above all, to have the court's vindication that it was unjust for Spanish Fork administrators to threaten her job because of her personal life. She was also pleased to recognize that the ruling could help other gay and lesbian teachers like her, by establishing a significant precedent against a school's efforts to restrain a teacher's private life.

Then she and her partner broke out a bag of Oreo cookies and made root beer floats for their seven children to celebrate their family's victorious fight to live free of discrimination. ▣

Birth *of a* Movement

Few people thought about equal rights for gay and lesbian people before June 17, 1969. The reason: Gay men and lesbians were commonly thought of — and commonly thought of themselves — as on the wrong side of the law, morality and mental health.

In many states, they could be arrested for having sex. Most religions considered homosexuality a sin. And the American Psychiatric Association designated it a mental disorder, something that was used as grounds to bar them from employment in the military, government and other professions. So deep was society's prejudice against gay men and lesbians that they risked being physically attacked, even killed, simply by revealing their sexual orientation. To protect their jobs, their safety and their lives, most gay men and lesbians chose to hide this aspect of their identities.

But on that summer night in 1969, something changed. First, law enforcement officials raided the Stonewall Inn, a gay bar on New York City's Christopher Street. Then they ordered everyone to line up and examined their clothing: Those wearing clothes thought inappropriate to their gender were rounded up, arrested and led outside to a paddy wagon. Those thought to be dressed appropriately were released.

Nothing up to this point was unusual. Raids occurred at the Stonewall monthly. But what was remarkable was that, this time, as the arrests were being made, people fought back. They shouted "pigs" at the police and threw bottles, cans and whatever they could find. Some rocked the paddy wagon; others escaped from it. And the next night, as word of the event spread, several thousand people came out and rioted again.

Indeed, after that night's spontaneous rioting, gay men and lesbians nationwide began to fight back against the forces that would define them as criminal, immoral and mentally ill — and they began to fight for equal rights. Although gay men and lesbians had stood up for their rights before the Stonewall riots, such occurrences were rare. The events that evening marked a turning point. Now gay men and lesbians were standing together in large numbers and refusing to be invisible any longer. It was the birth of a new civil rights movement.

The first significant step forward came just four years after the Stonewall riots, when the American Psychiatric Association rescinded its designation of homosexuality as a mental disorder. But the legal battles gay and lesbian people faced would prove much tougher.

As of the early 1960s, some form of law barring sexual relations between two people of the same gender existed in all 50 states. Gay and lesbian activists targeted these laws as unjust and succeeded in overturning many of them. But as of 2000, such laws remained on the books in 16 states, according to Lambda Legal Defense and Education Network.

Activists soon began to fight for laws that would bar discrimination on the basis of sexual orientation in employment, housing or education — much like the laws that prohibit discrimination on the basis of race, religion, gender or disability. But fewer than half the states had such laws by the close of the 20th century. And proposed federal legislation that would prohibit employment discrimination on the basis of sexual orientation still hasn't been made law.

More recently, activists have also turned to fighting for the rights of gay men and lesbians to serve in the military *(see "To Serve With Honor" on p. 136)*, to marry and to become parents. But while Vermont made history in 2000 by passing the first civil union law granting gay and lesbian couples the same rights as married heterosexual couples, as of the same year, 33 states and the federal government had passed laws prohibiting marriage between gay and lesbian couples.

There remains, in short, a very long way for gay and lesbian people to go to achieve equal rights under the law. But many are convinced that they will eventually succeed because, they say, they are on the side of what is right.

BECOMING AMERICA

by MARIA FLEMING

We hold these truths to be self-evident, that all men are created equal." The opening words of the Declaration of Independence marked the beginning of our nationhood. And yet they represent a destination, too. For despite this noble principle, the diverse peoples that the new nation comprised were profoundly unequal. Slowly but steadily, however, the sacrifice and persistence of women and men who believed in a principle larger than themselves have inched us closer to realizing our national ideal of equality for all.

Despite the tremendous progress we have made in the last two centuries, there is still a distance left to travel in achieving this ideal; inequities still plague our society. The legally sanctioned segregation of children in schools was struck down by the courts in 1954, yet in many parts of the country we still maintain a dual school system that is divided along the fault lines of race and ethnicity, with African Americans and some ethnic minorities often getting fewer and inferior educational resources.

We have corrected many of the discriminatory aspects of a justice system that allowed some states to deny African Americans the right to practice law, serve on juries and testify in court, and often subjected black men to the inhumanity of "lynch law." Yet justice is, in many respects, still a black and white issue in America. African Americans are often subjected to "racial profiling" by some law enforcement agents, who automatically consider black people suspect because of their skin color alone. Studies also indicate racial bias in the application of the death penalty. Black defendants, for example, are significantly more likely to receive a death sentence than white defendants in capital cases.

The quota system that favored immigrants of European descent over other ethnic groups was finally eliminated in 1965. Nevertheless, our current attitudes and public policies toward some immigrant groups are reminiscent of the strident nativism of the early 1900s.

Civil rights legislation passed in the 1960s and later decades protected most Americans from job discrimination based on an indelible characteristic such as race, gender or disability. As of the year 2000, however, lesbians and gay men in many parts of the country still had no guarantee that they could not be fired from their jobs simply because of their sexual orientation.

These are just a few of the challenges we still face as a pluralistic society struggling to live out our national creed. Moving beyond our country's legacy of bigotry and discrimination requires not only working to bring all of America's diverse groups to the table, but a willingness to sit down at the table together and honestly confront the hard truths of our past; to examine how that painful history has shaped our current public institutions, communities and attitudes; and to negotiate together a more just, more equitable, more harmonious future for all Americans.

Langston Hughes wrote many now-famous poems in which he expressed his hopes for the United States. In one poem, titled "Let America Be America Again," Hughes calls our nation "The land that never has been yet—/And yet must be." Indeed, our history can be read as our collective attempt to *become* the America described in our founding documents more than 200 years ago. As we continue to advance toward that goal, the lives of the men and women whose stories are told in this volume can serve as roadmaps for the journey. ⊠

CONTRIBUTORS

★ ★ ★ ★ ★ ★ ★

LISA BENNETT is the deputy director of FamilyNet, the Web site of the Human Rights Campaign. A frequent contributor to *Teaching Tolerance* magazine, she lives in Trumansburg, New York.

GARY COLLISON is professor of English at Pennsylvania State University. He is the author of *Shadrach Minkins: From Fugitive Slave to Citizen* (Harvard). He lives in York, Pennsylvania.

MARIA FLEMING is a former Teaching Tolerance staff writer. She is currently a freelance education writer and editor based in Brooklyn, New York. She develops supplemental curricular programs for Scholastic Inc. and has written more than 20 books for children and teachers.

BRANDON MARIE MILLER has written several books for middle-grade readers in the People's History Series (Lerner), including the award-winning titles *Buffalo Gals: Women of the Old West* and *Just What the Doctor Ordered: The History of American Medicine*. She lives in Cincinnati, Ohio.

BETH HEGE PIATOTE is a freelance writer and adjunct professor at the University of Oregon in the School of Journalism and Communication. Among the publications she contributes to is *Native Americas: Akwe:kon's Journal of Indigenous Issues* (Cornell). She lives in Eugene, Oregon.

HARRIET SIGERMAN is a historian and freelance writer based in Maplewood, New Jersey. She has written several volumes of the Young Oxford History of Women in the United States series, including *An Unfinished Battle: American Women 1848–1865* and *Laborers for Liberty: American Women 1865–1890*. She is also a contributor to Oxford's *American National Biography*.

"In Context" and "At Issue" sidebars were contributed by the following writers: "Equality Before the Law" by Louise Arkel; "Birth of a Movement," "To Serve With Honor" and "Storming the Barricades" (in part) by Lisa Bennett; "Reclaiming Lost Lands" (in part) by Beth Hege Piatote; "A Second Revolution," "Revolution Within a Revolution" (in part), "Reclaiming Lost Lands" (in part), "The Myth of the Melting Pot," "Property Values," "Segregation in the Far North," "A War on Two Fronts," "Get on the Bus" and "Rights and Wrongs" by Maria Fleming; "Rebel With a Cause" by Elizabeth Lloyd-Kimbrel; "Revolution Within a Revolution" (in part) by Harriette Gillem Robinet; "Starving for the Right to Vote" and "Struggle Within a Struggle" by Harriet Sigerman; "A Question of Faith" by Gene Smith; "Breaking New Ground" by Jim Carnes; and "Paper Trails" by Tim Walker.

FURTHER READING

★ ★ ★ ★ ★ ★ ★

For readers interested in finding out more about the events chronicled in this book, a list of some of the major sources used in researching the text follows.

Acuña, Rodolfo. *Occupied America: A History of Chicanos*. New York: HarperCollins, 1988.

Altfeld, E. Milton. *The Jew's Struggle for Religious and Civil Liberty in Maryland*. Baltimore: M. Curlander, 1924.

Appiah, Kwame Anthony, and Henry Louis Gates Jr., eds. *Africana: The Encyclopedia of the African and African American Experience*. New York: Basic Civitas Books, 1999.

Aptheker, Herbert. *A Documentary History of the Negro People in the United States*. New York: Carol, 1993.

Barnes, Catherine A. *Journey from Jim Crow: The Desegregation of Southern Transit*. New York: Columbia University Press, 1983.

Berson, Robin Kadison. *Marching to a Different Drummer: Unrecognized Heroes of American History*. Westport, Conn.: Greenwood Press, 1994.

Brown, Dee. *Bury My Heart at Wounded Knee: An Indian History of the American West*. New York: Henry Holt, 1991.

Cameron, Ardis. *Radicals of the Worst Sort: Laboring Women in Lawrence, Massachusetts, 1860–1912*. Urbana: University of Illinois Press, 1993.

Cole, Donald B. *Immigrant City: Lawrence, Massachusetts, 1845–1921*. Chapel Hill: University of North Carolina Press, 1963.

Collison, Gary. *Shadrach Minkins: From Fugitive Slave to Citizen*. Cambridge: Harvard University Press, 1997.

Cott, Nancy F., ed. *No Small Courage: A History of Women in the United States*. New York: Oxford University Press, 2000.

Duberman, Martin B. *Stonewall*. New York: Dutton, 1993.

Estep, William Roscoe. *Revolution Within the Revolution: The First Amendment in Historical Context, 1612–1789*. Grand Rapids, Mich.: Eerdmans, 1990.

Franklin, John Hope, and Alfred A. Moss Jr. *From Slavery to Freedom: A History of African Americans*. New York: Knopf, 1994.

—— and Loren Schweninger. *Runaway Slaves: Rebels on the Plantation*. New York: Oxford University Press, 1999.

Frost, Elizabeth, and Kathryn Cullen-Dupont. *Woman's Suffrage in America: An Eyewitness History*. New York: Facts on File, 1992.

Fuchs, Lawrence H. *The American Kaleidoscope: Race, Ethnicity, and the Civic Culture*. Hanover, N.H.: Wesleyan University Press, 1990.

Gaustad, Edwin Scott. *A Religious History of America*. New York: HarperCollins, 1990.

——. *A Documentary History of Religion in America*. Grand Rapids, Mich.: Eerdmans, 1993.

Gonzalez, Gilbert G. *Chicano Education in the Era of Segregation*. Philadelphia: Balch Institute Press, 1990.

Harding, Vincent. *There Is a River: The Black Struggle for Freedom in America*. San Diego: Harcourt Brace, 1981.

Isaac, Rhys. *The Transformation of Virginia, 1740–1790*. Chapel Hill: University of North Carolina Press, 1982.

Josephy, Alvin M., Jr. *Now That the Buffalo's Gone: A Study of Today's American Indians*. Norman: University of Oklahoma Press, 1984.

Kelley, Robin D. G., and Earl Lewis, eds. *To Make Our World Anew: A History of African Americans*. New York: Oxford University Press, 2000.

Marks, Paula Mitchell. *In a Barren Land: American Indian Dispossession and Survival*. New York: Morrow, 1998.

McClain, Charles J. *In Search of Equality: The Chinese Struggle Against Discrimination in Nineteenth-Century America*. Berkeley: University of California Press, 1994.

Miller, Neil. *Out of the Past: Gay and Lesbian History from 1869 to the Present.* New York: Vintage, 1995.

Nabokov, Peter, ed. *Native American Testimony: A Chronicle of Indian-White Relations from Prophecy to the Present, 1492–1992.* New York: Penguin, 1991.

Newton, David E. *Gay and Lesbian Rights.* Santa Barbara, Calif.: ABC-CLIO, 1994.

Olson, James S., ed. *Encyclopedia of American Indian Civil Rights.* Westport, Conn.: Greenwood Press, 1997.

Pelka, Fred. *The ABC-CLIO Companion to the Disability Rights Movement.* Santa Barbara, Calif.: ABC-CLIO, 1997.

Rawitsch, Mark Howland. *No Other Place: Japanese American Pioneers in a Southern California Neighborhood.* Riverside, Calif.: University of California Department of History, 1983.

Shapiro, Joseph P. *No Pity: People with Disabilities Forging a New Civil Rights Movement.* New York: Times Books, 1994.

Takaki, Ronald. *A Different Mirror: A History of Multicultural America.* Boston: Little, Brown, 1993.

———. *Double Victory: A Multicultural History of America in World War II.* Boston: Little, Brown, 2000.

———. *Strangers from a Different Shore: A History of Asian Americans.* New York: Penguin, 1989.

Terborg-Penn, Rosalyn. *African-American Women in the Struggle for the Vote, 1850–1920.* Bloomington: Indiana University Press, 1998.

Thomas, David Hurst, et al. *The Native Americans: An Illustrated History.* Atlanta: Turner Publishing, 1993.

Wheeler, Marjorie Spruill, ed. *One Woman, One Vote: Rediscovering the Woman Suffrage Movement.* Troutdale, Ore.: NewSage Press, 1995.

Wollenberg, Charles M. *All Deliberate Speed: Segregation and Exclusion in California Schools, 1855–1975.* Berkeley: University of California Press, 1978.

Wright, George C. *Life Behind a Veil: Blacks in Louisville, Kentucky 1865–1930.* Baton Rouge: Louisiana State University Press, 1985.

Zinn, Howard. *A People's History of the United States.* New York: HarperCollins, 1990.

TEACHING TOLERANCE

The Teaching Tolerance project, introduced by the Southern Poverty Law Center in 1991, provides teachers of all grade levels with practical resources to help them foster unity, respect and equality in the classroom and beyond. Through the generous support of the Center's donors, all Teaching Tolerance materials are made available free or at minimal cost to educators nationwide.

The cornerstone of the project is a semiannual magazine, *Teaching Tolerance,* that is mailed to more than 600,000 teachers in 50 states and more than a dozen foreign countries. EdPress (Educational Press Association) awarded the magazine its highest honor, the Golden Lamp, in 1995.

In 1992, Teaching Tolerance released *America's Civil Rights Movement,* a teaching kit comprising *A Time for Justice,* a 38-minute documentary video on the history of the movement; the text *Free at Last: A History of the Civil Rights Movement and Those Who Died in the Struggle;* and a teacher's guide. Targeted at secondary students, the *Civil Rights Movement* kit has been distributed to more than 80,000 schools. *A Time for Justice* received the 1995 Academy Award for best short documentary.

In 1995, Teaching Tolerance released its second video and text package, *The Shadow of Hate,* comprising a 40-minute documentary video on the history of intolerance in America; the text *Us and Them;* and a teacher's guide.

The third Teaching Tolerance kit, *Starting Small,* was released in 1997. This resource, designed to help teachers of young children promote tolerance and peace, comprises an hour-long video documenting exemplary classroom practices and a book of classroom narratives, commentaries and activities.

In December 2000, Teaching Tolerance released its fourth curriculum package, *A Place at the Table,* of which this text is a component. This kit, examining three centuries of progress in the struggle for equality, also includes a 40-minute video in which contemporary teenagers reflect on issues of identity, equality and community, and a teacher's guide.

For more information on the Teaching Tolerance program, contact:

Teaching Tolerance
400 Washington Ave.
Montgomery, AL 36104
Phone (334) 956-8374
Fax (334) 956-8484
www.tolerance.org

ACKNOWLEDGMENTS

The production and publication of this book were made possible by a generous grant from the Jeffry M. and Barbara Picower Foundation.

This book was produced by Teaching Tolerance, a project of the Southern Poverty Law Center. The project director was Jim Carnes. The editor was Maria Fleming. The design director was Rodney Diaz. The graphic designers were Russell Estes and Mary Neal Meador. Manuscript editors were Jennifer Holladay, Michelle McAfee, Cynthia Pon, Tim Walker and Elsie Williams.

Research assistance was provided by Stephanie Abdon, Naomi Bailey, Hershini Bhana, Jonathan Ebel, Roberta Pieczenik, Rowena Robles, Michelle Seldin and Mary Wyeth.

Picture research was provided by Sandi Rygiel and Pembroke Herbert of Picture Research Consultants, Inc., Topsfield, Mass.

Package design and original hand silkscreened artwork were provided by Julie Spivey and Scott Peek, Standard Deluxe, Inc., Waverly, Ala.

"I, Too," by Langston Hughes
From *Collected Poems,* by Langston Hughes
© 1994 by the Estate of Langston Hughes
Reprinted by permission of Alfred A. Knopf, a Division of Random House, Inc.

Grateful acknowledgment is made to the following individuals and organizations: Jewish Historical Society of Maryland; Copyright Clearance Center, Inc.; Harvard University Press; Stockbridge (Mass.) Library Association; Kentucky Department of Libraries and Archives; Filson Club Historical Society; National Archives; Julian Bond; Immigrant City Archives; American Textile History Museum; Moe Foner and the Bread and Roses Cultural Project, Inc.; Regional Oral History Office of the Bancroft Library; Western Historical Manuscripts Division of Huntington Library; Harold Harada; Mark Rawitsch; Riverside (Calif.) Municipal Museum; Riverside (Calif.) Public Library; Ronald Takaki; Sylvia Méndez; Joanie Sandoval-Méndez; Gilbert Gonzalez; Felix Rocha; Santa Ana (Calif.) Unified School District; Josephine Catalana; Billy Frank Jr.; Bill Couturiee; Judy Heumann; HolLynn D'Lil; Mary Jane Owen; Paul Longmore; the Fritson family; Wendy Weaver; Rachel Smith; the American Civil Liberties Union.

Teaching Tolerance was founded in 1991 to provide teachers with resources and ideas to help promote respect for differences. For more information, visit *www.teachingtolerance.org.* The Southern Poverty Law Center is a nonprofit legal and education foundation based in Montgomery, Alabama. The Center's co-founders are Morries Dees (Chief Trial Counsel) and Joe Levin (President and Chief Executive Officer). Its Vice-President for Programs is Richard Cohen. Its directors are Patricia Clark, Frances M. Green, Judge Rufus Huffman, Howard Mandell and James McElroy. ⊠

PICTURE CREDITS

FRONT COVER (top) Seaver Center for Western History Research, Los Angeles County Museum of Natural History; (middle) American Antiquarian Society; (bottom) *The Seattle Times*

2 (detail) Immigrant City Archives, Inc., Lawrence, Mass.

8 (detail) Greg Villet, LIFE Magazine (Time, Inc.)

10–11 Chicago Historical Society

12 Old Dartmouth Historical Society, gift of William F. Havermeyer, 1910

13 "Imaginary Landscape," artist unknown, Colonial Williamsburg

15 "A Philadelphia Anabaptist Immersion During a Storm," by Pavel Petrovich, The Metropolitan Museum of Art, Rogers Fund, 1942 (42.95.20)

19 (left) Boston Athenaeum; (right) Library of Congress

22–23 "Part II, The Fugitive, No. 19," by Jacob Lawrence, Hampton University Museum

24–25 Library of Congress

26 (top) Library of Congress; (bottom) Illinois State Historical Society

29 Courtesy Massachusetts Historical Society

30 Library of Congress

32 American Antiquarian Society

33 Library of Congress

34–36 The Filson Club Historical Society, Louisville, Ky.

37 Chicago Historical Society

38 Courtesy The Historic New Orleans Collection

39 Kansas State Historical Society

41 Library of Congress

42 (top) Wide World; (bottom) Corbis

43 Greg Villet, *LIFE* Magazine (Time, Inc.)

44 Don Clavens, *LIFE* Magazine (Time, Inc.)

46–47 "A Ponca Village," by Karl Bodmer, Courtesy of University of South Dakota Libraries

49–50 Nebraska State Historical Society

51 Edward E. Ayer Collection, The Newberry Library, Chicago

53 Smithsonian Institution

56–57 Lewis Hine, Library of Congress

58 Library of Congress

59 National Archives

60 "The Great Lawrence Strike," by Ralph Fassanella, Courtesy Mrs. Ralph Fassanella

61 Courtesy The Family of Carmella Teoli

62 American Museum of Textile History

63 Immigrant City Archives, Inc., Lawrence, Mass.

64 Immigrant City Archives, Inc., Lawrence, Mass.

65 *Industrial Worker*, March 21, 1912

66 Courtesy James S. Pula

68–69 The Granger Collection, New York City

70 *The Suffragist*, Oct. 16, 1915

71 (top) Wood Collection, The Huntington Library; (bottom) Library of Congress

72 Library of Congress

76 Stock Montage, Inc.

77 Library of Congress

78 (top) Collection of Janice L. & David J. Frent; (bottom) Schomberg Center, New York Public Library

79 Collection of Jancie L. & David J. Frent

80–84 Sumi Harada Collection

86 Courtesy Kate Whitmore

88 Archie A. Mayatake

90–91 Courtesy of the Mendez and Vidaurri Families

92 Corbis

93 Wide World

94 Courtesy of the Mendez and Vidaurri Families

95 Alaska and Polar Regions Archive, Rasmuson Library, University of Alaska, Fairbanks

96 Seaver Center for Western History Research, Los Angeles County Museum of Natural History

97 Institute of Texan Cultures

100–101 *The Seattle Times*

102 "The Last Salmon Run," by Alfredo Arreguin

103 Mark Harrison/*The Seattle Times*

104 (left) MSCUA, University of Washington Libraries, Neg. #NA1536; (right) Neg. #379

106 *The Seattle Times*

107 Corbis

108 Matt McVay/Saba

110–111 AP Wide World

112 HolLynn D'Lil

115 (top) HolLynn D'Lil; (bottom) AP Wide World

116 Photo by HolLynn D'Lil

117 HolLynn D'Lil

120–121 Nathan Bilow/Allsport

122 Eli Reichman for *USA Weekend*

124 Collection of Sally Fox

125 Courtesy Naomi Fritson

126 (top) Peter Read Miller/*Sports Illustrated*; (bottom) Lara Jo Regan/Gamma Liaison for *TIME*

127 Courtesy Sue Mounsey

128 Jim Edgecombe/*Minden Courier*

130–133 Courtesy Wendy Weaver

134 (top) Courtesy Wendy Weaver; (bottom) Mark Pett/*City Weekly*

136 Patsy Lynch

139 Jason Olson/*The Daily Herald*

BACK COVER (top) Lewis Hine, Library of Congress; (bottom) Schomberg Center, New York Public Library

INDEX

References to illustrations and their captions are indicated by page numbers in **bold.**

Abolitionists, 17, 22–**25**, 26–33, 78
Act of Toleration, 17
Aetna Insurance Company, 31
African Americans, 22–33, 34–45, 67, **78**–79, 84–85, 97–99, 142
Alabama, **42**–45
Alaska, 20, 55, **95**
Alcatraz Island, 105
Alien land laws, 82, 85–86, 87–88
Altfeld, E. Milton, 17
Amendments, constitutional, 11, 20, 30, 32, 37, 44–45, **70**–79, 88–89
American Civil Liberties Union, 135, 137
American Coalition of Citizens with Disabilities, 114
American Disabled for Attendant Programs Today, 114
American Federation of Labor, 61–62
American Psychiatric Association, 141
American Revolution, 19, 28
Americans with Disabilities Act, 114, 119
Anglican Church, 11–**13**, 17–19, 50
Arizona, 82, 93
Arkansas, 78
Ashley, John, 28–29
Ashraf, Mian, 21
Asian Americans, 62, 67, 80–89, 98–99
Athletics, **120**–29, **132**, 138
Auberger, Michael, 114

Baptists, 11–20
Battle of the Little Bighorn, 55
Baxter, John George, Jr., 42
Bigelow, Ann and Francis, 31
Birmingham, Ala., 42
Black Codes, 37, 44
Blackwell, Elizabeth, 127
Blue Lake, N.Mex., 55
Boldt, George, 107–9
Boston, Mass., 22–32
Boston Vigilance Committee, 27–29

Boycotts, 40, **43**–44
Brom and Bett v. *J. Ashley, Esq.,* 29
Brotherhood of Sleeping Car Porters, **36**–37
Brown, Henry "Box," **32**
Brown v. *Board of Education,* 45, 98, 136
Burn, Harry, 73
Burns, Anthony, 32
Burns, Lucy, 75
Burton, Phillip, 116

Califano, Joseph, 114, 117–18
California, 80–98, 110–18
Cammermeyer, Margarethe, 136–37
Canada, 25, 31–32
Carter, Jimmy, 114, 117–18
Casper, Dean, **122–23**, **125**, 127
Casper, Sarah, **122**–29
Catholics, 17, 50
Center for Independent Living, 119
Cherokee Indians, 54
Cheyenne Indians, 48
Chicanos, **90**–99
Child labor, **57–59**, 66
Chinese Exclusion Act, 82
Cicero, Ill., 84
Citizenship, U.S., 55, 67, 81–**84**, 85–86, **88**, 89, 96, 99, 109
Civil disobedience, **42**, 105
Civil Rights Act, 45, 114
Civil Rights Movement, 35, 40, 42–45, 85, 99, 138, 141
Comanche Indians, 48
Compromise of 1850, 24
Congressional Union, 71–72, 74
Constitution, U.S., 11, 16, 20, 30, 53, 70, 109. *See also* Amendments
Craft, William and Ellen, 27, 28
Craig, Hugh H., 88
Craig, Lewis, 12–13
Crook, George, **51**–54
Cruz, Luisana, **126**
Curtis, George W., 124

Day, Dorothy, 75
Disability rights, 110–19

Douglass, Frederick, 27, 72
Du Bois, W. E. B., 45
Duncan, Carey, 41
Dundy, Elmer S., 52–55

Education, 90–98, 106, 121, 142
Education Amendment Act, 114, 121
Emancipation, 28–29, 35
Emerson, Ralph Waldo, 54
Employment discrimination, 131–40
Equal Rights Party, 77
Estudillo, Miguel, 86
Ettor, Joe, 61, 63–64

Fasanella, Ralph, **60–61**
Field, Sara Bard, **70**–79
Fishing rights, 100–109
Fox, Robert, 36, 38, 40, 45
Fox, Samuel, 36, 38, 40
Frank, Billy, Jr., 102–9
Franklin, Benjamin, 33
Frank's Landing, Wash., 100–109
Freedom Riders, **42**
Freeman, Elizabeth, 28–**29**
Fritson, Naomi, **122**–29
Fugitive Slave Law, 22–32

Galles, Kristen, 128
Gays, 131–42
Gender discrimination, 120–29
Geronimo, 47
Gnade, Carol, 135
Gompers, Samuel, 62
Grant, Ulysses S., 48
Grimes, Leonard, 30
Gruening, Ernest, 95

Habeas corpus, writ of, 52
Hamlet, James, 25
Handler-Klein, Steven, 118
Hansler, J. C., 86
Harada, Jukichi, **82–86**, 88
Harada, Ken, **83–84**, 86
Harada family, 80–86, 88
Hartford Courant, 31
Hawaii, 20
Hayden, Lewis, 25–28, 30–32

Health, Education, and Welfare, department of, 112–18
Heumann, Judy, **112**–18
Hilton, Matthew, 139
Hope, John, 37
Housing, 48, 59, **63**, 84–85, **93**
Houston, Tex., 44
Howard, E. A., 50–51
Hughes, Langston, 142
Hutchinson, Anne, 14

Immigrants, 56–67, **80**–99, 142
Independent Living Movement, 119
Indiana, 77, 78
Indian Religious Freedom Act, 20
Indian Removal Act, 54
Indian Self-Determination and Education Assistance Act, 106
Indian Territory, 48–49, **51**–52, 54
Industrial Workers of the World. *See* Wobblies
Internment camps, 87–88, 99
Islamic Center of New England, 21
Italian Americans, 57–**61,** 63

Jackson, Jesse, 67
Japanese American Citizens League, 97
Japanese Americans, 62, 80–89, 97, 99
Japanese-Mexican Labor Association, 62
Jefferson, Thomas, 20
Jenkins, Bruce S., 140
Jennings, Elizabeth, **39**
Jewish Congress, 97
Jews, 16–17, 40, 84, 97
Jim Crow laws, 39, **41–42,** 44–45
Jones v. *Mayer,* 85
Joseph, Chief, 47, 52

Kemble, Edward, 48–49
Kennedy, Thomas, **16**–17
Kent, James L., 96
Kentucky, 34–44
Kindberg, Maria, 72
Kindstedt, Ingeborg, 72, 74
King, Coretta Scott, 138
King, Martin Luther, Jr., 40, 45, 138
Ku Klux Klan, 38, 108

Labor history, **36–37,** 56–67
Lakota Indians, 55
Lambertson, G. M., 52–53
Land settlements, 55
Latimer, George, 24
Lawrence, Mass., 56–67

Lay, Benjamin, **33**
League for the Physically Handicapped, 119
League of Freedom, 26, 31
League of United Latin American Citizens, 97
Lesbians, 131–42
Leschi, Chief, **104–5**
Lizarras, J. M., 62
Lockwood, Belva Ann, 77
Loguen, Jermain W., 25
Louisville, Ky., 34–**36,** 38, 40–44

Madison, James, 19–20
Maine, 55
Major, Richard, 18
Marcus, David, 94–95
Marshall, Thurgood, 97–98
Maryland, 16–17
Massachusetts, 14, 21, 22–32, 56–67
Matlovich, Leonard, 136–37
McCormick, Paul J., 96
Méndez family, 93–98
Méndez v. *Westminster,* 98
Mexican Americans, 62, 67, **90**–99
Michigan, 78
Migrant workers, **92–93, 96**
Military, U.S., 51, 99, 136, 141
Miller, Frank, 86
Miller, George, 116
Minden, Nebr., 120–29
Minkins, Shadrach, 24, 29–32
Milton, Mass., 21
Montgomery, Ala., **43**–45
Mormons, 132, 137
Morris, Robert, 29
Mounsey, Tara, **126**
Moyer, Jeff, 112, 115
Muslims, 21

National American Woman Suffrage Association, 71, 73–74, 78–79
National Association for the Advancement of Colored People, 40, 45, 85, 97–99
National Association of Real Estate Boards, 85
National Association of the Deaf, 119
National Federation of the Blind, 113, 119
National Gay and Lesbian Task Force, 138
National Organization of Women, 116, 119, 129
National Origins Act, 63
National Urban League, 40, 45

National Woman's Party, 74–75
National Women's Law Center, 128
Native peoples, 20, 46–55, 67, 95, 98–109
Nebraska, 46–54, 78, 120–29
New Mexico, 93
New Orleans Daily Picayune, 31
New York, 25, 39, **66,** 74, 78, 113, 141
Nez Percé Indians, 52
Niagara Movement, 45
Niobrara River, Nebr., 46–54
Nisqually Indians, 102, **104**–6
North Dakota, 78
North Star, 72

Oberlin, Ohio, **26**
Office of Civil Rights, 123–24, 128
Ogle, Joel, 96
Ohio, **26,** 78
Oklahoma, 48, 51
Omaha, Nebr., 51–52, 54
Oppenheim, James, 65
Orange County, Calif., 93–98
Oregon, 70, 82, 87, 102, 105
Osborn, Ron, 126
Osceola, 47
Owens, Mary Jane, 112, 118

Pacific Northwest, 50, 52, 100–109
Parks, Rosa, **42,** 45
Passamaquoddy Indians, 55
Paul, Alice, 75
Pearce, Horace, 36, 38
Penobscot Indians, 55
Plessy, Homer, **38**
Plessy v. *Ferguson,* **38,** 44–45, 96–98
Polish Americans, 57, 60, 63, **66**
Ponca Indians, 48–55
Poppleton, Andrew, 52–53
Posca, Sherm, 126
Presbyterians, 16, 18, 50
Puritans, 14

Quakers, 18, 33
Quincy, Mass., 21

Reconstruction, 36–38, 43–45
Reed, James, 18
Reservations, Indian, 48, 51–52, 54, 105
Rhode Island, 14, 78
"Ride-ins," 41–42, 45
Riley, Elizabeth, 31
Riverside, Calif., **80–86,** 88
Robinson, Cynthia, 85–86, 88
Rocco, Angelo, 60–61, 67

Roosevelt, Franklin D., 88, 99
Runaway slaves, 22, **24–32**
Russell, John, 36
Russian Americans, 58, 63

Sands, Larraine, 139
San Francisco, Calif., 89, 110–18
Schenck, Alberta, 95
Schuyler, George, 99
"Section 504," 114, 119
Sedgwick, Catherine, 29
Sedgwick, Theodore, 29
Segregation, 34–45, 84–85, 90–99
Seneca Falls, N.Y., 69, 72, 79
Separate Baptists, 11–20
"Separate but equal," **38,** 45, 96–98, 117
Sexual orientation, 131–42
Sharon, Mass., 21
Sheffield Declaration, 28–29
Shelley v. *Kraemer,* 85
Sims, Thomas, 32
Sioux Indians, 48, 55
Sit-ins, 105, 110–18
Sitting Bull, 47
Slave catchers, **24–25,** 27–28
Slavery, 13, 17, 22–33, 37
Slovak League of America, 63
Smith, Rachel, 131–35, 137–**40**
South Dakota, 55
Spanish Fork, Utah, 130–40
Spotsylvania County, Va., 10–20
Standing Bear, Chief, 48–**49,** 50–55
Standing Bear v. *Crook,* 53–55
Starr, Barry, 21

Stevens, Isaac, 103, **104–5**
Stevens, Thaddeus, 43
Stevenson, Adlai, 84
Stonewall riots, 141
Stowe, Harriet Beecher, 26
Strikes, 60–67
Supreme Court, U.S., **38,** 44–45, 55, 77, 84–85, 88–89, 96, 97–99, 104–5, 108

Taft, William Howard, 66
Taos Pueblo Indians, 55
Tecumseh, 47
Tennessee, 73
Teoli, Carmella, 58–**61,** 66
Texas, 93
Tibbles, Thomas Henry, 51–52
"Title IX," 114, 121, 123–**26,** 128
Trail of Tears, 54
Transportation, **34**–45
Treaties, Indian, 48, **52,** 100–109
Truman, Harry S., 99

Underground Railroad, 23, 31
Unions, labor, **36–37,** 61–67, **116**–17
Utah, 130–40

Van Buren, Martin, 54
Vassar College, 124
Vermont, 141
Vernon, Mabel, 72
Vidaurri family, **94**
Virginia, 10–20, **30,** 75
Virginia Statute for Religious Freedom, 20

Voting rights, 37, 45, 68–79, 99
Voting Rights Act, 45

Wadley, Robert, 133–**34**
Walker, David, 27
Walker's Appeal, 27
Waller, John, 12–13, 15, 17–19
Ward, John H., 38, 40
Warren, Earl, 98
Washington, D.C., **116**–18
Washington state, 82, 100–109
Weaver, Wendy, **132–40**
Webster, John L., 52–53
Wells-Barnett, Ida B., 79
Western states, 70, 72, **77,** 82
Westminster, Calif., 90–98
White Eagle, Chief, 48, 51, 54
Whitman, Walt, 67
Williams, Roger, 14
Wilson, Woodrow, 70, 74–78
Winchell, Barry, 137
Winthrop, John, 14
Wisconsin, 135
Wobblies, 61, 63–65
Woman suffrage, **68–79.** *See also* Voting rights
Wood, Charles Erskine Scott, 79
Wood, Laurie, 138
Workers, 56–67, **92–93, 96**
World War I, 74, 78, 97
World War II, 88, 99
Wortham, Doug, 135

Yakama Indians, 104
Yick Wo, 89